Hope is Like the Sun

"Hope is like the sun, which, as we journey toward it, casts the shadow of our burden behind us."

~ Samuel S. Smiles, Author (1812-1904)

Hope is Like the Sun

Finding Hope and Healing
After Miscarriage, Stillbirth, or Infant Death

Lisa Church

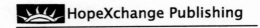 HopeXchange Publishing

Hampton, Virginia

HopeXchange Publishing
26 Towne Centre Way #731
Hampton, VA 23666-1999, U.S.A.
www.HopeXchange.com

Cover design and photos by Michelle Allen.
Printed in the United States of America

10 9 8 7 6 5 4 3 2 1

Library of Congress Catalogue Number: 2004100996

ISBN 0-9748699-6-1

Dedication

To the child I carried, but never knew: I loved you from the start, and I will remember you always.

To the women and their families who face the grief and pain of pregnancy loss. May the words that follow bring you comfort and hope.

Contents

Acknowledgements

A work of non-fiction is a collaboration of research, review, and the unselfish contributions of others. Such a project leaves many to thank.

Velicia, Anna, Kathy, and Julia: your courage, honesty, and dedication made this book possible. My deepest respect and appreciation goes to each of you.

To the editors who gave their time and expertise; your involvement made my passion a reality. Thank you Sandy Goodman, Casey Curry, Lorraine Call, Naved A. Jafri, M.D., F.A.C.O.G., and Thomas A. Bender, PA-C, who dedicated himself to reviewing the medical information.

A special thanks to Ann Prescott for giving her time, passion, and expertise to this book. Authors Tom Golden and Sherokee Ilse also made important contributions despite their demanding schedules.

Penny Davis consulted tirelessly on the cover design, and Kim Matthews graciously lent her industry expertise to this project. Suzanne DeWitt conducted a thorough proofreading.

My heart and my heartfelt thanks, belong to my husband Mark for his enduring love and support.

Thank you all.

Foreward

At least one out of four reported pregnancies ends tragically with the loss of the baby. Since pregnancy loss is not an unusual event, the natural assumption might be that bereaved parents have access to many supportive resources, and that those around them would respond with compassion and understanding. Sadly, it has been my experience that appropriate support and helpful resources are inadequate. Too many well-meaning individuals feel that the best way to cope with the loss is to "*move on*," "*forget about it*," and "*just try again*;" advice which is presented freely and all too often.

In *Hope is Like the Sun*, Lisa Church offers a "mini-support group" in book form. Drawing from her own experience with miscarriage, as well as the losses of her friends, she gives down-to-earth, insightful advice and supportive information to bereaved parents and those who care for them.

Through personal narratives, she illustrates the many facets of the normal grieving process that accompany pregnancy loss. This book presents user-friendly suggestions for coping with a wide range of emotional responses, assuring women that these reactions are "normal" and not "crazy." It includes sound information about good self-care and the importance of maintaining physical health while healing emotionally.

Hope is Like the Sun offers health care professionals, family members, and friends, insights about the grief that follows the loss of an unborn child. Those who have suffered pregnancy loss will find comfort and support here; and most of all, they will feel the hope and encouragement that can only come from one who has "been there." ~ **Ann H. Prescott, RN, MSEd, CT; Grief Counselor, Certified in Thanatology**

A Word From the Author

We all face loss. I was clearly reminded of this as I worked on the final phases of this book. While completing my edits, Hurricane Isabel slammed into the Outer Banks of North Carolina and then swept through my home, on the east coast of Virginia.

Almost two million people were impacted by the force of the storm. Each one felt the loss that can only result from an "act of God." A loss of safety, electricity, gasoline, ice, clean drinking water, and scores of trees and branches.

Waterfront communities were hit especially hard when the tidal surge sent three to six foot waves rushing down local streets. Sections of homes were swept away, while the houses and businesses that remained filled with water.

Raging winds entangled trees in power lines and rooftops. Rising flood waters saturated carpets and furniture, while smaller items were set adrift.

In the massive clean up that followed the storm, mounds of debris were left piled in front of every home, telling a story of what was lost. Many of the materials of life were ruined - gone forever. More than forty people experienced the ultimate loss at the hands of Hurricane Isabel; they lost their lives.

We all face many types of loss during the course of our lives. We may loose jobs, possessions, love or money; yet we go on. The loss of a loved one, however, is not so easily handled.

One of the most difficult types of loss is the death of a child. To a parent, the loss of a child, at any age, seems to defy the laws of the nature. Parents are not designed to outlive their children; when they do, they face an unbearable grief.

The loss of a baby during pregnancy may be the most misunderstood form of loss. While the parents struggle to mourn their child without any memories to cling too, society robs their opportunity to grieve. As a result, parents are forced to face their pain in silence.

My baby died in the 12th week of life. Before I could hold him, meet him, or see his tiny face, he was gone. And yet, I had spent those three months loving him.

I was in a daze after the loss, and for weeks I found it difficult to talk about. As I began to open up and share my experience with others, I was shocked to discover how many people around me had felt the pain of miscarriage.

To my dismay, I found that four of my close friends, women I had known for years, had each suffered a miscarriage. Even though it happened before I knew them, it felt strange to know that they had silently carried this burden.

This book shares our stories, five individual journeys from grief to healing. Our experiences were very different, but our paths converged at a place where hope emerges, and life can go on.

If you are reading this book because you, or someone you love, has suffered the death of a child, please accept my deepest sympathy. I hope that you will find information, comfort, truth, encouragement, and healing in the pages that follow.

Please understand that reading this book, or any book, will not remove your loss, but it is a step in the right direction. May your steps begin today.

Disclaimer

This book is intended to provide information about the subject matter covered. It is sold with the understanding that the publisher and author are not engaged in rendering medical, psychological, or any other professional services. If medical, psychological, or other expert assistance is required, locate the services of a competent professional.

It is not the purpose of this book to reprint all of the information that is available on this topic, but to complement, amplify and supplement other texts. For more information, refer to the many resources listed in the Appendix.

Dealing with loss and grief is a difficult task. Anyone experiencing grief should expect to spend time and tremendous effort working towards the healing process.

Every effort has been made to make this book as complete and accurate as possible. However, there may be typographical and/or content errors. This text is intended to be a general guide and is not the ultimate source of miscarriage and grief information. Furthermore, this book contains information on pregnancy loss and grief only up to the printing date.

The purpose of this manual is to educate and entertain. The authors and publishers shall have neither liability nor responsibility to any person or entity with respect to any loss or damage caused, or alleged to be caused, directly or indirectly by the information contained in this book.

If you do not wish to be bound by the above, you may return this book to the publisher for a full refund.

Chapter 1

Miscarriage: You Are Not Alone

*I*t still amazes me that almost everyone I know or meet has been affected by a miscarriage in some way. It surprised me that women I had known for years had been carrying this silent burden, and I had no idea. After my pregnancy loss, countless women began to reveal the bond we shared; they had suffered a miscarriage too.

Our society has great difficulty dealing with grief and loss, and in many ways this traps victims of pregnancy loss. When I suffered my miscarriage I entered a 'quiet' realm, surrounded by others who endured the pain of their loss in silence.

This book examines the journey from grief to the eventual healing of miscarriage. It is a path that I unfortunately shared with four close friends. Pregnancy loss brought us together in a sorrowful, but profound way. Our experiences with grief were completely different, but the pain we felt was dreadfully similar. This book will share our journeys, five passages from painful beginning to hopeful end.

My Journey Begins...

My husband and I had been married for 10 years before I felt ready to have a baby. I wanted everything to be perfect, and finally, it was. Our first baby was due in May of 2000.

Just before Halloween, I began spotting. At first I panicked, but after talking with the doctor I felt a little better. He said this happens sometimes and it is not always serious.

Since I was already 12 weeks along, and I had not experienced any problems, the doctor felt that I was most likely going to be fine. He scheduled an ultrasound for the following day, just to be sure.

The next morning my light spotting had become heavier. I had an ominous feeling that bad news was coming.

During the ultrasound, the technician stared intently at her screen. She seemed to be looking for something that was not there. Her words confirmed what I already knew inside...there was no heartbeat.

The tears began streaming down my face as my husband helped me sit up on the table. I felt dazed as the technician left the room and gave us a few minutes to collect ourselves. I dreaded leaving that room... and facing a world without my baby.

Velicia

" It was in 1991, January 25th. I was unaware that anything was wrong, except that I was spotting a little...After being examined, the doctor said that I had an infection and that I may lose the baby.

After arriving at the hospital I was examined again and told that because the 'sac' had ruptured, from a small *tear, an infection had set in. They would have to induce labor. We were 25 weeks along.*

The nurse was extremely nice and gave me morphine to ease whatever pain I would feel. I think it was more to dull the after effects of losing a child. I remember being asked before the birth if I wished to hold the baby... what a stupid question.

Most of the rest is a haze. I remember someone telling me it was girl, then changing it to a boy, as at that age the genitals are very small. I held him...and accepted this had really happened. I held him and cried after I realized he wasn't sleeping."

Anna

" I was about 9 weeks along and had some spotting, which was, of course, alarming. I called the OB GYN, who asked about any other symptoms I may be having, such as cramping, which I didn't. Sadly, this gave me hope.

I was scheduled the following day for an ultrasound. The technician looked for a few minutes. The fact that she didn't say anything for a couple of minutes worried me. At that point, I sort of knew what she was going to say. Then she said that she was not able to find the heartbeat.

And the tears just started rolling. And I remember calling my husband and telling him. And I remember calling my boss and telling him I wouldn't be coming back to work that day."

Julia

"The miscarriage happened sometime after [my third child] was born in April, 1970. ...I had a feeling I was

pregnant, but wasn't sure. It's hard to describe, but I just felt I had conceived.

I didn't go to the doctor to confirm, I just wanted to see what would happen. Something did...

I passed the baby one night and had to go to the hospital."

Kathy

"My first one happened in the 10th week, as did my second. In both cases, things seemed to be fine and during the 10th week, I noticed spotting.

I contacted the doctor as soon as this happened and was advised this can sometimes happen, so if it gets worse, contact the doctor.

For the first one, the spotting started on Thursday, and the following Sunday was more than spotting. The doctor had me immediately go to the emergency room, and she determined that I was having a miscarriage.

The second time, as soon as the spotting started she had me in the office and I had an ultrasound. They determined that the fetus was not as it should be, and once again, I was having a miscarriage."

If you have found yourself dealing with the grief and pain of pregnancy loss, you are not alone. Miscarriages seem to happen almost routinely, however they are anything but routine for the parents and their family.

Miscarriage – The Facts

My doctor handed me a tiny, black leaflet after finding that my baby's heart was not beating. It contained a few, small pages of vague information. That was all I to explain the death of my baby. I still have the pamphlet, and I keep it to remind me of the reason I wanted to write this book

During a time when you need it the most, information about miscarriage to seems to be sparsely provided by doctors, hospitals, and health care workers. This can cause frustration, confusion, and even guilt about the possible causes of a pregnancy loss.

Sadly, miscarriages are a common occurrence. Although statistics can vary slightly from one source to the next, here is a general account (based primarily on information provided by the March of Dimes) of the frequency of miscarriages in the United States:

- There are about 4.4 million confirmed pregnancies in the U.S. every year.
- 900,000- to 1 million of those end in pregnancy losses EVERY year.
- More than 500,000 pregnancies each year end in miscarriage (occurring during the first 20 weeks).
- Approximately 26,000 end in stillbirth (considered stillbirth after 20 weeks)
- Approximately 19,000 end in infant death during the first month.
- Approximately 39,000 end in infant death during the first year.
- Approximately 1 in 4 pregnancies end in miscarriage; some estimates are as high as 1 in 3. If you include loss that occurs before a positive pregnancy test, some estimate that 40% of all conceptions result in loss.
- Approximately 75% of all miscarriages occur in the first trimester.
- An estimated 80% of all miscarriages are single miscarriages. The vast majority of women suffering one miscarriage can expect to have a normal pregnancy next time.
- An estimated 19% of the adult population has experienced the death of a child (this includes miscarriages through adult-aged children).

The numbers tell the sad story of how often pregnancies end in loss. However, society and the medical community do not often seem to provide the proper response to support the high rate of loss that occurs each year.

Why Did it Happen?

When a baby is created, it takes half of its genes from the mother's egg (that ovulated that month) and the other half from the father's sperm. At the exact moment of conception, all of the genes mix and come together.

Sometimes errors occur when the genes combine and important information is lost. This is a common cause of miscarriage, and about 50% of the time there is no explanation- other than terribly bad luck. From this point on, there is no chance for a healthy pregnancy.

When the missing information is needed and it is not there, the baby dies and you begin to miscarry. If the lost information is not needed for many weeks, the pregnancy will continue as normal until that time. When a miscarriage does not happen right away, it is called an IUFD (intrauterine fetal demise) or a "missed abortion," and it may not happen for some weeks later.

Do not confuse the word abortion with the term that describes the elective procedure, which is called a "therapeutic abortion." The word "abort" simply means "to end prematurely," so abortion and miscarriage are medically interchangeable terms. Doctors refer to a miscarriage as a "spontaneous abortion."

Miscarriages can also occur if the baby does not plant itself properly into the womb lining. This is another common cause of pregnancy loss that is the result of bad luck. Infections, inherited genetic disease, hormonal imbalances and problems with the uterus or cervix, such as large fibroids, are not as common, but they are all conditions that can cause miscarriages.

There are many reasons women experience pregnancy loss, and they are not usually causes that could have been prevented. Most of the time it is chance and the odds went against the pregnancy.

Working too hard, drinking a glass of wine or forgetting to take folic acid are NOT contributing factors to a pregnancy loss. Miscarriage is simply nature's way of making sure a baby has the best chance of survival; it is survival of the fittest. However, suffering a miscarriage does not mean that a woman will never be able to have a healthy baby.

My pregnancy seemed completely normal from the start. I had morning sickness and all of the expected symptoms. Everything seemed fine. My baby's heart never started beating, and yet my body went on for many weeks more, with no change in symptoms at all. My doctor later explained that I had high hormone levels that continued the pregnancy symptoms. Velicia also recalled:

> *"I was unaware that anything was wrong, except that I was spotting a little after I had been stooping, cleaning out leaves around the outside of our house."*

However, some women notice that morning sickness and other symptoms do not occur or they begin to lessen. Anna described it this way:

> *"I hadn't felt some of the 'typical' pregnancy symptoms and this had already worried me. At times, I didn't really 'feel pregnant' because I didn't have those symptoms. I think, in some way, I was suspicious from the beginning that something wasn't right."*

No matter what the cause of a miscarriage, it is important to accept that some things have no explanation, and sometimes there is nothing to blame.

Was It My Fault?

The myths and misinformation regarding the causes of miscarriage can cause incredible guilt for a woman whose pregnancy abruptly ends. The sometimes sparse information provided by doctors and health care professionals does not always do an adequate job of reassuring a woman that she is not to blame.

There are a number of myths surrounding pregnancy loss and what can cause it. Here are some common ones that do NOT cause a miscarriage:

- **Lifting small children or something heavy**. In general, healthy pregnant women may lift 15-20 pounds *in moderation*. For women in the second or third trimester, heavy lifting should be avoided because it can cause a strain in the ligaments that hold the uterus in place. Even if you were to experience such a strain, you would feel intense pain, but it would not necessarily cause a miscarriage. Chances are that your body would cause you to drop a heavy item before any harm could occur.

- **Stress or working too hard**. Many women experience stressful events during pregnancy, and they have perfectly healthy babies in spite of the trauma. Countless others continue their normally hurried work pace without slowing down, and while they may feel tired, they are not at risk of a miscarriage.

- **Drinking alcohol.** Some women agonize over the cocktails or glasses of wine they drank before they knew they were pregnant. A newly forming baby receives so little of its mother's blood for the first few weeks of pregnancy, that this should not be a cause for concern. To continue drinking throughout the pregnancy however, can cause a serious problem called Fetal Alcohol Syndrome. Although it may not be a cause of miscarriage, it is important to avoid alcohol during pregnancy.

- **Bad eating habits.** Forgetting to take your prenatal vitamins or failing to eat properly will generally not hurt your baby- it will hurt you. Your body will rob from you what it needs for the baby, and you will feel the effects. Failing to get enough of the food or nutrients that your baby needs can cause low birth weight and other developmental problems for the baby. However, poor eating habits will not cause miscarriage.

- **Falling, or getting kicked or hit in the stomach.** In most cases, your baby is so well protected in amniotic fluid, that only you would be hurt during a fall or blow to your stomach. You should always seek medical attention if this occurs, but generally these events (especially when they happen in the first trimester) do not cause pregnancy loss.

- **Car accidents.** Again, it is normally you and not your baby who becomes injured in a car accident. Unless your stomach and uterus become punctured, or you experience a period of time when your heart or breathing stops, it is unlikely that your baby would die.

- **Sex.** Lovemaking has no adverse effects on your baby. You may experience spotting after sex, but this is simply because your cervix is very soft and the blood vessels are very prominent and dilated. Unless you have been instructed by your doctor to refrain, there is no reason for concern.

- **Exercise.** Working out can actually have benefits for you and your baby if you follow a few simple rules. Never exercise to the point that you feel faint or exhausted, and decrease any weights used by one-third. Do not raise your heart rate excessively; since acceptable ranges vary by person, your doctor can determine your limit. This is not a miscarriage factor, but overdoing it can reduce the amount of oxygen the baby is getting.

Having a good understanding of the true causes of a miscarriage can leave you feeling more at ease about the reason your pregnancy loss occurred. It can be hard to accept, but in many cases there is simply no tangible explanation, and certainly not anything that you contributed to.

What Does Cause a Miscarriage?

Considering the long list of myths that many people believe to be causes for miscarriage, you may be left wondering about the real causes. Outside of the errors that nature imposes, there are a few conditions that can contribute to early pregnancy loss. Those are:

- **A multiple pregnancy** (triplets, quadruplets, quintuplets, etc.)
- **Age**. For women under the age of 35, the average miscarriage rate is about 6.4%. That rate more than doubles to 14.7% for women who are 35-40. For women over 40, the miscarriage rate jumps to 23.1%.
- **Poorly managed diabetes**. For women with well-controlled diabetes, there is no increased risk of miscarriage.
- **Scleroderma**. A soft tissue disease that affects the internal organs and causes a stiffening of the skin. This condition is not overly common.
- **Lupus**.
- **Antiphospholipid Antibody Syndrome**. A disease involving the immune system.
- **Smoking**. It is estimated that cigarette smoking increases the risk of miscarriage by 30-50%, and it may also be a contributing factor to SIDS (sudden infant death syndrome).
- **Occupational exposure to solvents or toxins** (such as arsenic, lead, formaldehyde, benzene and ethylene oxide) is known to increase the risk of miscarriage.
- **Certain medications** such as methergine, methotrexate, and mifepristone.
- **Certain infections.** Note that common colds, viruses, etc. do not cause miscarriages.

It is important to note that sexually transmitted diseases such as Gonorrhea and Chalmydia increase the risk of ectopic pregnancies (which occur outside the uterus, most commonly in the fallopian tubes). These infections, as well as infections that occur after therapeutic abortions, scar the tubes, making pregnancy difficult and increasing the chances of ectopic pregnancies.

Therapeutic abortions performed after sixteen weeks pose a greater threat of miscarriage during future pregnancies. This is due to a higher risk for infection and complications when compared to abortions performed before eight weeks. There is no evidence of *physical* problems related to earlier term abortions and their effect on future pregnancies; however there can be emotional factors, which could cause problems.

Avoiding possible causes of miscarriage when considering or planning for your next pregnancy is important. Especially focus on those that you can control such as quitting smoking, treating genital infections, refraining from recreational drug use, and controlling diabetes.

It is also known that previous use of the contraceptive pill slightly reduces your risk of miscarriage. However, I had used the pill for years, and still suffered one.

There are no guarantees in pregnancy, we already know that, but it is important to avoid anything that increases the risk of miscarriage.

Will I Ever Be Able to Have a Baby?

After pregnancy loss, many women feel plagued by the worry that they will never be able to have a healthy baby, especially if their miscarriage occurred during their first pregnancy. The good news is that the odds are in your favor.

Approximately 90% of women who have had one miscarriage, go on to have a normal pregnancy and a healthy baby next time. I am a part of that 90%. I had a textbook pregnancy my second time around and a perfectly healthy baby girl.

An estimated 60% of women who have suffered two miscarriages have a healthy subsequent pregnancy. Even for women who have three miscarriages in a row, there is more than a 50% chance of a healthy baby in the fourth pregnancy.

The decision to get pregnant again can be a simple assumption or a cause for intense anxiety and stress. We will discuss this topic in detail in Chapter 16: *Trying Again.*

For now, it is important for you to know that you are not alone. Over half of all miscarriages are caused by chromosomal errors that are completely out of our hands.

A majority of the others are caused by unknown health conditions, hormone problems, infection, or a poorly formed placenta- not by anything you personally did. Don't listen to ANYONE who tries to tell you differently.

Chapter 2

Facing Your Loss

*I*n simple terms, grief is a person's individual reaction
to a loss, however grief is anything but simple. All loss can
be painful and each type carries with it a unique set of
issues. One of the greatest losses that can occur is the
death of a loved one.

It is only in recent years that parents were thought to
be capable of caring deeply for their unborn babies. The
research of two pediatricians in the 1970's proved that
emotional attachment actually begins very early in
pregnancy.

A woman who suffers a miscarriage experiences a very
specialized type of loss. From the very day she finds out
she is pregnant she begins to form a bond with her
unborn baby. This sense of 'oneness' magnifies the loss
when a miscarriage occurs.

There is no set time for grief to take place. As a parent,
you never entirely get over the loss of your baby. However,
it is generally noted that grief can last between 6 months

and 4 years. That does not mean that the pain is over when the grief is over, it means that you have been able to accept your loss and move toward healing.

Grief is often described in a number of phases or stages. There is no particular order to grief, but there are reactions that commonly occur. You may experience some or all of them. You may find that you skip from one feeling to the next, or you may experience one aspect of grief only to return to a previous one. Grieving is an individual process, and there is no right or wrong way to grieve.

It is important to understand that there is no set pattern to grief, no expected phases or order that will always occur. Each person will have a unique and very personal grief experience.

Various sources describe the 'stages' of grief using a number of different terms. They are described using several different names, however the basic idea is the same.

Typically they include:

- **Shock and numbness.** When the loss first occurs it may feel that you are in 'a fog.' This gives you time to prepare to accept loss.
- **Feeling the pain of loss.** After the fog has lifted, you begin to experience the pain of the loss. This includes *physical, emotional, social* and *spiritual* pain
- **Recovery and acceptance.** As you begin to accept your loss and how it has changed you and your family, the healing process begins. You incorporate your baby's memory into your lives and form new hopes and dreams.

It is important to know that you can and will move through grief and into healing. Understanding the grieving process can help you feel empowered and give you comfort and encouragement.

Healing from grief means accepting your loss and how it has changed you and your family. It means investing in a new future, while finding ways to remember the child from your past.

The loss of your baby will affect your entire being-mind, body, and soul. You will experience a wide range of reactions that we will examine more closely over the next few chapters. Recognizing the emotions of grief and exploring suggestions that can help you deal with them is an important part of the healing process.

"Between the grief and nothing I will take grief."
~ *William Faulkner*

Chapter 3

Shock and Numbness

*I*n the same way that your body uses shock and numbness to handle physical trauma, your brain uses it to deal with emotional trauma. The loss of a child is certainly a traumatic experience. All of the plans and dreams you had for your child and your family are unexpectedly shattered.

Shock and numbness are nature's way of cushioning the blow, allowing our minds to prepare for the emotions to come. This state can last just a few minutes or stretch on for weeks.

Hearing the News

I received the news that my baby had died during an emergency ultrasound. Immediately, tears started streaming down my face. I felt stunned and it was difficult to move. I was in a daze. Everything seemed to be going in slow motion and it almost felt 'surreal.'

For weeks after that, I felt an eerie numbness that disturbed me. Although I knew that I loved my husband and my family, I was almost unable to experience any real feelings. At times I worried about how long this would last and wondered when I would be able to feel deep emotions again.

Kathy also said that she felt shock upon hearing the news of her first miscarriage and explained:

"We had just made all the plans to move our first child to another bedroom and had picked out the wallpaper."

Velicia, however, recalled a slightly different emotion:

"I didn't feel shock, just an unbearable, insatiable feeling of aloneness. I called my mother and talked to her, and she cried with me. I remember holding my husband's head because he was crying...At that time, I felt completely disassociated from everything that was going on around me."

What to Expect

During this time you may experience a variety of feelings and emotions including:
- Things may not 'feel real.'
- You may feel panic or bewilderment.
- You may find it hard to concentrate or make decisions.
- You may withdraw from others.
- You may feel empty or numb.
- You may feel restless.
- You may burst out crying or feel unable to control your emotions.

In mid-term or late losses, a mother may hear "phantom crying" or feel kicking in her womb after delivery. These sensations are normal and they can be intensified by grief for weeks following the loss.

All of these are normal reactions to traumatic loss. While experiencing these feelings, you may want to avoid making major decisions or seek help and advice from someone you trust. Also keep in mind that accidents can be more likely to happen when you have difficulty concentrating. This does not mean you should withdraw from society, just be aware of times that you may want to ask for assistance.

Shock and numbness usually last for a brief time, however, like any reaction, they can reoccur during the grieving process. It is simply the brain's way of protecting our fragile emotions and preparing for what comes next. After the shock and numbness wear off, the real grieving will begin.

"Every heart has its own ache."
~ Thomas Fuller

Chapter 4

The Physical Pain of Grief

*E*xperiencing a traumatic loss affects every part of us. When an emotional injury occurs the body often expresses physical symptoms as well. Taking care of the physical you will not erase your grief, but it will help you feel better and offer a welcomed distraction.

Physical Symptoms of Grief

Sobbing, crying, sighing, and weeping are all common to those facing loss, and they are normal signs of physical grief. Some studies show that these are necessary releases of sadness, and suppressing them can cause physical effects such as poor memory, sleep disturbances, lack of concentration, reduced appetite, insomnia, and even abuse of alcohol and drugs.

Allowing yourself time to cry, sigh, and even sob is important to your emotional, as well as your physical, well-being. As adults, we often feel the need to be strong and hold back our emotions, but physical health can be affected by repressing these feelings.

There are several physical symptoms that Medical Doctors and Psychologists have identified as common to grief:

- Tightness in the throat
- The feeling of choking or suffocation
- Heavy feeling in the chest or chest pains
- Tension and headaches
- Absent mindedness
- Reduced muscular power
- Shortness of breath
- Empty feeling in the stomach
- Sighing

These events are physiological or biochemical reactions to your grief. At times, grief can have major physical health consequences such as a compromised immune system. This condition can leave you susceptible to illnesses that can require hospitalization; even surgeries can be more common among those in grief.

Your physical well-being becomes very important during the grieving process. At a time when you will feel very little energy or motivation, you will need to focus on your physical health. Pay special attention to your eating and sleeping habits, exercise, and be sure to get plenty of human contact. These steps will be critical to your physical health while dealing with loss.

Nutrition

Your eating habits can become very unstable during grief. You may have little appetite, depleting your body of the vitamins and nutrients it needs.

On the other hand, you may find yourself eating more to comfort yourself. This can lead to unwanted weight gain, which can make you feel sluggish or even angry with yourself. You may also find yourself eating sugar and fatty foods that can drain your body of energy.

While dealing with my loss, food was my consolation and drug of choice. Although I tried to make healthy eating choices, I struggled to lose the weight I had gained during my pregnancy. The unwanted pounds seemed to remind me of my loss.

Maintaining healthy eating habits will help your mind and body feel better and give you the energy you need to heal.

Here are some simple suggestions:

- **Eat plenty of fresh fruits**, vegetables, and grains.
- **Cut down on sweets** and junk foods.
- **Add vitamins and minerals** if your diet is not well balanced.
- **Find healthy foods you like** that are easy to fix.
- **Try eating smaller meals several times a day** rather than three big ones.
- **Drink lots of water**. Try to drink eight 8-ounce glasses every day.

Grief inhibits the trigger for thirst, so you may forget to drink, which can lead to dehydration. You will need to focus on drinking the water your body needs, even when you do not feel thirsty.

Sleep

Now more than ever, your body needs the healing process of sleep. The proper amount and quality of sleep is vital in restoring and refreshing your body.

Your sleep patterns may become disrupted during grief, especially in the beginning stages. You may have trouble sleeping, or you may find yourself sleeping more than usual to avoid the pain of your loss.

If you are having trouble sleeping try these suggestions:

- **Avoid caffeine** or reduce your intake of coffee, colas, tea, and even chocolate.
- **Stick to a routine**. Get up and go to bed at the same time every day.

- **Read a book before bedtime**. If a novel keeps you up, find a boring book.
- **Be sure the room temperature is comfortable**- not too hot or too cold.
- **Stick to quiet activities** the last hour before bed.
- **Avoid heavy meals before bed** that can disrupt sleep.
- **Turn off radios, TV, etc**. The noise can affect the quality of your sleep.
- **Exercise for 20-30 minutes at least 4 hours before bedtime**. Be sure not to exercise close to bedtime- your body will still be 'hyped up.'
- **Drink warm milk**- yes it really does work. Plain milk is a natural sedative.
- **Take a warm shower** or relaxing bath before bed.
- **Try deep breathing** and relaxation techniques while lying in bed.
- **Visualize a quiet and peaceful place**.
- **Avoid alcohol and sleeping pills**. These are only temporary fixes that can lead to dependency and other issues later on.

Exercise

At a time when your energy levels are down it can be difficult to think about exercise. However, routine physical activity promotes better health, increases fitness and causes the body to function better. It also cleanses the body, energizes you and relieves stress. Exercise not only reduces stress hormones, it also triggers the release of hormones that cause a feeling of well-being.

Here are some tips to help you get started:

- **Consult your doctor** before starting any exercise program. Inform your physician about what is happening in your life and ensure that your health is closely monitored.
- **Realize that your reaction time and coordination may be reduced** during grief.
- **Find an exercise you like!** It does not have to be a typical exercise- dancing, swaying to music,

gardening, yard work, and even household chores can be great physical activities for your body.
- **Set aside time** to exercise regularly.
- **Turn routine tasks or errands into exercise.** Take the stairs instead of the elevator, walk to the store, or park far away from the entrance.
- **If the weather is nice, enjoy the outdoors**. Fresh air and sunshine are great for lifting your spirits. Taking a walk down the street, jogging through the park, or running on the beach can be a great way to exercise and feel better.

Human Contact

Having contact with another person is a physical need during grief that can be overlooked. Touching, hugging, and holding another person is both comforting and healing.

Here are some great ways to connect with others:
- **Hold hands** with your spouse or a close friend.
- **Hug and play with children.**
- **Cuddle pets.**
- **Get a massage.**
- **Have a manicure** or pedicure.
- **Have your hair washed** and styled at a salon.
- **Hugs.** When you need a hug- ask for one!

Focusing on your physical needs will not chase away your pain, but it will make you feel more prepared to handle your loss. Set time aside to plan and focus on your physical well-being.

If you are having difficulty deciding where to begin, ask someone you trust to help you prioritize your health needs. And be sure to get a hug while you're at it!

Questions to Ask Yourself

When experiencing the physical pain of grief, consider the following questions:

- **Have I informed my doctor** about what is going on in my life?
- **Am I practicing healthy eating habits?** Could I be doing better?
- **Am I getting enough sleep?** Too much sleep?
- **Am I getting any exercise or physical activity?** Could I improve?
- **Am I getting enough human contact?**

If these questions have caused you to identify areas you would like to improve, decide on at least two actions you will take to address each one.

Use this space to write them down:

_____

_____

_____

_____

_____

_____

_____

_____

_____

_____

_____

_____

_____

_____

Chapter 5

The Emotional Pain of Grief

*D*ealing with a pregnancy loss and the grief that follows is a very individual experience. There is no order or schedule for grieving, however there are feelings that many people share.

For a woman who has suffered a miscarriage, the emotional connection to the loss is a huge one. For many, emotional pain constitutes the very heart of grief.

A woman sees the child she carries as a part of herself, and when that child dies, a part of her dies as well. This leaves a great feeling of emptiness and loss that is not experienced in the same way by others. This can compound the emotional reaction women have to their pregnancy loss.

There are many feelings that are associated with the emotional pain of grief. You may experience some or all of them. You may find that you have certain feelings briefly, while others are much more intense and may even reoccur. There is no specific pattern to grief, but there are common emotions that often occur.

Guilt

When a normal, seemingly healthy pregnancy is interrupted by a miscarriage, it is almost impossible for the mother not to ask herself, "Was this my fault?" The question can be brief or overwhelming.

Just before finding out about the loss of our baby, I knew in my heart that the news was not going to be good. I was preparing my husband and through my tears telling him, "I know I did everything right. I took my vitamins, I drank orange juice, I did everything I was supposed to..."

My husband in no way blamed me for what was happening. I was reassuring myself that the baby's fate was not my fault.

Velicia described her intense feelings of guilt by saying:

"I believed it was my fault for having been outside working...murderer."

And Anna recalled similar feelings, saying:

"One of the first things I said to the Doctor ...was that I had been working too hard. I was blaming myself."

On the other hand, Julia said:

"I never felt any guilt."

In some cases, simple education or reassurance from the doctor can be enough to quiet feelings of guilt. My doctor explained that many times miscarriages are 'nature's way' of preventing a child that has some type of genetic defect. This did give me comfort- to know that these things sometimes just happen, seemingly without an external cause.

Kathy also shared a similar experience and recalled:

"I felt that I had perhaps not taken care of my body the correct way- I had a drink when I did not know I was expecting, or did not eat the right way. I also remember saying 'How will I handle a two year old, new baby and a job?' So I had thought perhaps because of my negative thoughts, it caused a miscarriage.

I don't have the guilt (now) and that is due to my doctor. At the times of the miscarriage we talked about how sometimes there are issues with the fetus or something else, and even though it hurts, and it is not something you want to happen- it is for the best."

Anna's doctor also reassured her and she described that:

"The doctor quickly and gently corrected me and explained that there were actually a number of things that could cause a miscarriage- but that it was not working too hard. He explained briefly a few things that could be the cause- his reassurance really did help."

However, for some guilt is not so easily resolved. Guilt is an emotion that is not usually satisfied with explanations- even those of qualified physicians. Guilt can leave you feeling helpless because there is no hope of resolving it; you cannot bring your baby back.

Velicia described her battle with guilt by saying:

" I had two other children who I distanced myself from as much as possible. I had caused the death of their brother, no matter how unintentional, and therefore wasn't fit to be their mother."

Guilt can cause a number of different feelings and reactions. You may have low self-esteem and feel that you are 'less of a person.' You might think that you have disappointed your spouse or family for not producing a healthy baby. Kathy experienced this reaction, recalling that:

"I felt that I had failed my husband, son and family."

41

You may even believe that God is punishing you for something that happened in the past. Velicia described that:

> *"The depth of the emotion I felt caused me to remember some very unpleasant things that had happened when I was a teenager, and in my grief, I thought I was being paid back for being so careless. It was a scary time."*

Grief can become even more complicated when there are intense feelings of guilt. For some the guilt is never resolved, and it never goes away. This can leave people with emotional baggage they carry for the rest of their lives.

Extreme guilt that goes unresolved can lead to more serious problems and disrupt the healing process. Guilt that continues for a long period of time can actually lead to health problems and cause psychosomatic illnesses. It is important to stop blaming yourself and allow the healing process to continue. Velicia explained that:

> *"Guilt is not God's way of helping us to heal, rather something we impose upon ourselves to hide from our own forgiveness, which is hardest to give."*

Healing Guilt

It is critical to accept the guilt you feel, even if it is unreasonable. Taking this important first step will allow you to understand and deal with your guilt.

If you are experiencing guilt, here are some suggestions to help you handle it:

- **Be honest** about the guilt you feel. Admit it and ask yourself why you feel that way.
- **Talk about your guilt** with a trusted friend or counselor.
- **Remember that sometimes there is no explanation** for loss, so there does not have to be something or someone to blame.

- **Try speaking directly to the child who died**. Place an empty chair in front of you, or hold a doll, and tell him/her what you need to say.
- **Forgive yourself!** Realize that no one is perfect. If you feel the need, ask loved ones and even God to forgive you.
- **Try writing in a journal** or simply jot down thoughts about your guilt.
- **Get help**. If your own efforts to cope with your guilt are not enough, do not be afraid to seek professional help.

Remember that many people who have faced loss and grief experience feelings of guilt. In most cases the guilt will subside as you focus on it and give yourself the time you need to understand and deal with it.

Questions to Ask Yourself

Here are some questions to consider as you work through your guilt:

- **Do I feel guilty?** Why?
- **Am I determined to place blame** or find a reason for my miscarriage? Why?
- **Have I forgiven myself?** Do I need to ask others to forgive me? Who?

If these questions have uncovered guilt that you are experiencing, write about it now.

Use this space:

_____

_____

_____

_____

_____

_____

Next, determine two actions you will take to address the guilt you are feeling.

Use this space to write them down:

_____

_____

_____

_____

_____

_____

_____

_____

_____

Anger

As you begin to deal with your loss, it is normal to feel angry and even abandoned. You may feel angry toward the baby who died, your doctors, your family, or even God.

While many direct their anger at others, you may also feel angry with yourself. This type of anger is also manifested as guilt.

When I decided I was ready to have a baby, it seemed like everything in my life had fallen into place. I had just moved into the house I wanted- ideal for raising a child. I had a stable job that I loved, with great health benefits. I was finally ready.

The first month we tried, I got pregnant. It was all so perfect... almost too perfect. Three months into my textbook pregnancy, the baby died. Everything was shattered. I told myself, "Serves you right to think it would all work out so perfectly-you dummy..."

I was angry that the innocence and beauty of having a baby was stripped away. I was angry that something I yearned for and planned for was gone. And I was mad at myself, that I did not produce a healthy baby.

Anna described a different type of anger, saying:

"I wasn't angry about the miscarriage itself, but I did feel somewhat angry with my husband afterwards. I didn't feel like it impacted him the way it did me."

And Velicia described a similar experience when she said:

"Initially I was angry at myself, but after that, my husband."

While some women feel anger toward family members, others experience anger or envy towards other mothers. My mother often shares an encounter she had soon after having me, and my twin sister. While pushing the two of us in a stroller, she was abruptly approached by a woman in a department store. The woman sharply said that it wasn't fair that my mother had TWO healthy babies, and she couldn't even have one. Apparently, the woman had recently had a miscarriage, and she was experiencing intense anger.

While some struggle with anger during their grief, others may not. Kathy reported that she did not recall feelings of anger, and Julia agreed, describing that:

"I never felt anger- I just wondered how I'd gotten pregnant, because I was using an accepted method of birth control."

During grief, it often appears that men more easily express anger, while women more often express sadness. You may notice that the men around you are displaying anger. This can be a common reaction for a man feeling the pain of loss.

Like grief, anger shows itself in very different and personal ways. It may cause you to feel restless and impatient. It can even cause physical reactions such as heaviness, or pain in your chest.

No matter how you experience anger, it is vital that you find healthy ways to express it. Holding in anger can affect your well-being and prohibit the healing process.

Healing Anger

Connecting with and expressing the anger felt during grief is an important step towards the healing process. Unresolved anger can lead to negative or pessimistic thoughts, becoming easily agitated, or even upsetting others to relieve your own anger.

Anger can be a difficult emotion to handle. Here are some steps you can take if you are feeling angry:

- **Write a letter** to the person you feel angry with: yourself, your baby, your spouse, a family member, or even God.
- **Talk to a close friend** or a professional about the anger you are feeling.
- **Find a healthy outlet** for your anger such as punching a pillow, intense exercise, screaming aloud (not at another person), or even running around the block as fast as you can.
- **Help another person**. Use your restless energy to clean someone's house, mow a lawn or fix a meal for someone in need. Focusing on others is a great way to take your mind off your pain.
- **Cry**. Many women (and even men) release their anger through tears.
- **Confront the source of your anger**. If you are angry with a spouse or family member have an honest discussion during a time when you are NOT feeling angry. If needed, ask a close friend or professional to help.
- **If you are angry with God or your baby,** face an empty chair and have a 'confrontation,' expressing your anger.

Feeling anger as a part of grief is a perfectly normal reaction to your loss. Resolving that anger is an important step toward healing.

Questions to Ask Yourself

If you are feeling angry, consider the following questions:

- **Who am I angry with**? Why?
- **Have I confronted the source of my anger?** Who or what is it?
- **Do I have a healthy outlet** for my anger?

If you have discovered feelings of anger, decide on two actions you will take to resolve them.

Use this space to write them down:

_____

_____

_____

_____

_____

_____

_____

_____

_____

_____

_____

_____

_____

_____

Depression

When the reality of what you have lost sets in, depression and hopelessness may follow. At this point in grief we become surrounded by the loss and we feel powerless to overcome it. Velicia described that:

> "My grief was unlike anything I'd ever felt. It was all encompassing, and relentless in its greedy ownership of all I did or touched."

Anna remembered a slightly different experience, saying:

> "At the time I didn't think I was depressed, but looking back, I probably was. Maybe not depression as much as just grief."

Kathy described similar feelings saying that she did not have depression:

> "... as much as sadness."

Julia had a slightly different reaction describing her inner turmoil, She said:

> "I wanted the baby one minute, and then the next minute I didn't want another baby."

Depression can be one of the darkest times during grief. Feelings of sadness may dominate your emotions. You may feel hopeless, unable to enjoy anything, uninterested in sex, irritable, anxious, worthless, and you may even wish you were dead. You may have difficulty concentrating or making decisions, and you could find yourself unable to cry even when you want to.

Your body also reacts to the crushing force of depression. You may experience insomnia, sleep disturbances, poor memory, tension, fatigue, or changes in appetite.

During this time you may also feel lonely and have a yearning for your baby. You may feel cheated or haunted because you have no memories of your baby to comfort you.

I experienced an overwhelming feeling of wanting to be with my baby. I did not feel I could share it with anyone because I was worried they would think I was crazy. Velicia experienced similar feelings saying:

> *"I felt unsteady, emotionless and then too filled up, pent up, and at some point I wanted to be with [my baby] Shelby."*

While Julia said:

> *"I felt sad and wished many times over that maybe the baby could have been born. I did in a way miss the baby."*

During this time your feelings of loss may come in waves. You may feel fine one moment, and the next moment, find yourself in tears. Your depression may reoccur during times when surroundings or events remind you of your loss. You may even notice that simple items that remind you of your baby can set off feelings of sadness. Kathy described this when she said:

> *"At times I still have sadness when I see a newborn or think about how our child would be with this group or could be doing this now."*

My sister and I were pregnant at the same time, and our babies were due just four months apart. What was at first a joyful time for both of us, had turned to sorrow for me. I was at work when I got the call that she was in labor. Of course I was happy for her, but my emotional reaction to the news took me by surprise. As I hung up the phone, I suddenly found myself sobbing in the middle of my office.

For many, depression and sadness is the most painful part of grief. It is not unusual to have difficulty making the simplest decisions, to lack motivation, or to experience impaired judgment. The trauma of loss can also cause an emotional upheaval that triggers other memories from the past.

Velicia explained her experience with past memories saying:

> *"At one point I thought, because I had remembered things long forgotten, that I was losing my mind."*

Some studies have shown that women who suffer miscarriages are more likely to suffer symptoms of anxiety, nervousness and obsessive thoughts about what they might have done wrong, or worries about not being able to get pregnant again. The risk of experiencing a depressive disorder was also shown to be higher in certain studies that compared women who have had a miscarriage to those (in the same community) who had not.

As painful and difficult as depression can be, normal grief does begin to lift with the passing of time. As the depression passes, that is where true acceptance of your loss occurs and real healing can begin.

Healing Depression

Sadness, hopelessness and depression can be one of the hardest parts of grief. Getting through this critical time is difficult, but it can actually make way for healing.

Here are some suggestions when you are coping with depression:

- **Resist the temptation to be alone!** Do not cut yourself off from others. You need them now more than ever.
- **Connect with the ones you love**. Feeling love and support from family members, friends, your spouse and God can help.
- **Pray and meditate**. Read positive books, articles, and quotations.
- **Stay busy**. Discovering a new hobby, taking a class, or volunteering and helping others can keep

you from slipping into inactivity. They also keep your mind off of your grief.

- **Return to work**. If you have not already done so, returning to a productive and structured workday can help to alleviate depression. This safe environment can provide friendly support as well as a feeling or returning to 'normal.' Day-to-day tasks will also distract your mind from grief.
- **Keep a journal**. Writing down feelings that are too difficult to speak into words can be both cleansing and healing.
- **Stay away from excesses** such as alcohol, excessive eating, illegal drugs, overworking, or promiscuity. These things are only temporary escapes, and they can be harmful to your physical and emotional well-being.
- **Don't be afraid to ask for help**! If you have several symptoms that persist for several weeks, get professional help immediately. There are treatments and medications that can help. If you experience *any* suicidal thoughts call 911 immediately.
- **Remember that better days are coming**. When you are facing the very heart of grief, try your best to focus on moving toward your future.

There is no timetable for a person to move through depression. No one can say how quickly or slowly you should overcome it. You may not be able to get your life back on track as quickly as family and friends feel that you should.

It is important that you take steps to handle the depression when it comes, and focus your sights on brighter days. It may not feel like it, but they are just ahead.

Questions to Ask Yourself

If you are experiencing sadness or depression consider the following questions:

- **Am I depressed?**
- **Have I taken adequate steps to relieve my depression?** What are they?

If you have determined that you need to take further steps to combat depression, decide on two actions you will take.

Use this space to write them down:

_____

_____

_____

_____

_____

_____

_____

_____

_____

_____

_____

_____

_____

_____

_____

_____

_____

_____

_____

_____

_____

Chapter 6

The Social Pain of Grief

*T*oday's society is not comfortable with the topics of death and grief, making the grieving process one of solitude and misunderstanding. We live in a culture that has not accepted death, nor does it allow its people to openly grieve.

Whether it is the boy who was told not to cry, or the adult who feels that grieving is self-pity or selfishness, we are part of a society that is not equipped to cope with loss and grief. We learn to hide or control our feelings. In fact, many feel that these topics are 'off limits.' As children, many of us learn that grief is taboo, and grieving is to be done alone.

What Will People Think?

You may find yourself feeling embarrassed or reluctant to share your pain with others. You may also worry that you will be viewed as weak by opening up your emotional wounds to others. No wonder we find it so difficult to grieve!

After my pregnancy loss, I was concerned that those around me would think I was weak if they saw the depth of my pain. They had all moved on with their lives, yet I was still grieving. I was too embarrassed to admit it, and as a result I struggled through some difficult times alone. Julia described her experience this way:

> *"During the 70's no help was available to get through a miscarriage like there is now. There was sympathy of course from everyone, but other than that, there was no other emotional help given."*

Dealing with a pregnancy loss can be extremely frustrating because it is not widely viewed as the death of a child. Society will often expect parents to quickly bounce back and just 'have another one.'

In many ways our culture is simply not taught to acknowledge the pain of a miscarriage. It is not indifference, but lack of knowledge that creates this situation. As a result, parents are often not 'allowed' by society to grieve the loss of their baby.

Velicia recalled a similar experience explaining that:

> *"Those around me expected me to bounce back. They told me stories of women who birthed babies while working in the fields and strapped the baby on their backs and went back to work. Of course that served nothing except to make me feel even more inadequate. What a weakling I was... I thought."*

What Now?

You may feel that those around you have moved on, before you have worked through your grief. They may make you feel that you are taking too long to recover, or that you are holding on to your pain.

It is important to understand that many people have never experienced grief and they have no idea what you are going through. You are entitled to grieve, even if those around you do not understand.

It is not uncommon for people to quickly change the subject rather than discuss your loss. Remember that they are not intentionally trying to hurt you; in most cases they simply do not know what they should say or do.

This reluctance to talk about your baby may leave you feeling isolated and alone. Rather than retreat into solitude, here are some suggestions to try:

- **Seek out those who are comfortable talking about your grief.** Find a friend or family member who is able to deal with intense emotions.
- **Look for others who have faced pregnancy loss**. They may be people in your own circle of friends, or others you find in a chat room or online community.
- **Cry when you need too**. If you are concerned about what others think, then set aside private time each day when you can be alone and release your tears.
- **Realize that no one completely understands** how you felt about your baby.
- **Tell others how they can help**. Do not leave them guessing what your needs are.
- **Let others know if you need time to yourself** so they will not feel rejected. This is especially important with children.
- **Consider getting a pet**. They can make great companions if you chose one that fits your lifestyle.
- **Find support** by seeking out support groups, churches, online communities, and counselors. These can all be great sources of help and there is an extensive list of resources in the back of this book.

As you deal with the pain of your loss, it is important to be able to reach out to others. Although society may make that more difficult, it is worth the effort to find the support you need.

Questions to Ask Yourself

Consider the following questions:
- **Have I isolated myself?** Why?
- **Do I have someone I can talk openly with about my grief?** Who?
- **Have I connected with others who have experienced pregnancy loss?** How?
- **Have I told others how they can help me?** When? How? Who did I talk with?

Are you reaching out to others during your grief? Write about it now:

_____

_____

_____

_____

_____

_____

_____

_____

_____

_____

_____

_____

_____

_____

_____

_____

If you have identified some areas that need focus, consider at least two actions you will take to address them.

Use this space to write them down.

_____

_____

_____

_____

_____

_____

_____

_____

_____

_____

_____

_____

_____

_____

_____

_____

_____

"Out of suffering have emerged the strongest souls;
the most massive characters are sheared with scars."
~ E. H. Chapin

Chapter 7

The Spiritual Pain of Grief

*F*acing a major loss usually causes us to confront or even reconsider our basic beliefs about God, religion, death, and the afterlife. Some may turn to God for strength and comfort, while others find themselves questioning the religious beliefs they have known all of their lives.

Even those who have no religious upbringing may feel angry with God, or abandoned. Everyone responds to loss differently, but it almost always forces us to confront questions we may have been avoiding...about death...about God...about ourselves.

I can still remember the first time I went to church after my miscarriage. I have always loved going; the music and the service have always left me feeling recharged. But now it was different. I felt totally numb. I was unable to 'feel,' and it took weeks for that to wear off.

Velicia described a disconnected feeling, saying:

" I had never been 'religious,' never raised that way, but I believed in a Higher Power. ...At that point, I was unconnected from my faith."

While Julia recalled:

"I felt God was taking care of me and the baby I lost."

Why God?

Many times a traumatic loss will leave parents feeling like they have been shaken to the core. It is these times that cause one to examine what is inside. In the depths of grief you may feel yourself doubting God. Regardless of your religious beliefs, it is common to ask 'Why God?' when tragedy strikes.

While some are left angry and questioning how God could allow this to happen, others find that their faith can actually be deepened during such a time.

A belief in God is not a guarantee against pain and suffering. Death is an unavoidable part of life; and faith can be there to help us get through our losses, but it cannot prevent them.

You may have conflicting feelings about the God you love, because you feel He has failed you. If you continue to have unanswered questions, your pastor, rabbi, or priest can offer help.

What Now?

If you have been left feeling that you are spiritually shaken, it does not mean that something is wrong with you or your faith. Faith is not an insurance policy against doubt, fear, or frustration. It is there to help us deal with those feelings and give us the comfort and strength we need. Julia described that when she said:

"My faith, and the belief that someday I would see this child again, helped me handle the loss."

Kathy explained a similar experience when asked what comforted her, she responded:

> *"Talking with God to help me understand what happened and thanking him for the son we [already] had...and taking it one day at a time."*

In a time of grief, it is common to struggle with our faith and beliefs. It can be helpful to be reminded that we live in a world in which tragedies happen, and sometimes there is no reasonable explanation when loss occurs.

When I felt myself being tested, I had a decision to make, and mine was to reach out to God. In my times of doubt I found a verse that was encouraging and I repeated it anytime I felt angry or depressed. It gave me an action to take against my grief, it made me feel connected to God, and it lifted my spirits.

I memorized the verse so I could have it on hand any time I felt discouraged:

> *"So do not fear, for I am with you; do not be dismayed, for I am your God. I will strengthen you and help you; I will uphold you with my righteous right hand."* - Isaiah 41:10 (Holy Bible, N.I. V.)

Only you can decide what choice you will make when you feel yourself being tested. Remember that new faith often grows from grief.

Here are some suggestions:

- **Consider talking to a minister, priest or rabbi.** Counseling can be comforting and it can help you find answers to your questions. It may even renew your faith.
- **Explore and question your values and beliefs**. This process will strengthen some beliefs that you have known in the past and it may even form new ones.
- **Make time in your day for prayer and meditation.** This can be a great source of comfort and encouragement.

- **Draw strength from your faith and others during this time**. Think of your loss and grief as part of life's uncertainties that challenge us.

Grief affects every aspect of our being- body, mind, and soul. As you work through it, take the opportunity to embrace your values and beliefs and let them guide you to healing.

Questions to Ask Yourself

Here are some questions to consider:
- **Have I explored my values and beliefs?** What are they?
- **Have I set aside quiet time in my day?** Do I use this time to pray, meditate, or contemplate my beliefs?
- **Do I have a source of strength to lean on during difficult times?** What (or who) is it?

If these questions have helped you to consider your values and beliefs, write about them now:

_____

_____

_____

_____

_____

_____

_____

_____

_____

_____

If the questions you have just answered helped you to identify focus areas for your life, decide on two to three actions you will take to address them.

Use this space to write them down:

"There is no rainbow without a cloud and a storm."
~ *J. H. Vincent*

Chapter 8

Recovery and Acceptance

*A*fter the shock and numbness of your loss lifts and you experience the incredible pain of grief, you begin to move toward recovery, and the acceptance of a life without your baby. Of course you will never forget your child, and you and your family will find ways to incorporate remembrances of the baby into your lives. Your life will return to an altered state of 'normal.'

During this time you will find that you begin to enjoy life once again. Slowly, you begin to feel that the storm is passing and turmoil is gradually replaced with peace, and hope for the future.

I realized that I was starting to feel better when I could tell others about my loss without holding back tears. It became easier to talk about my baby.

How Do I Recover?

Experts have identified four 'tasks' that must be completed in order to work through the grief process. Accomplishing these goals will lead you to the closure of your grief and the beginning of healing:

1. **Accept** the reality of your loss
2. **Experience the pain** by allowing yourself to grieve.
3. **Adjust** to a new life without your child
4. **Emotionally relocate your baby** and move on with life.

Accepting the Reality of Loss

It can be difficult for parents to accept what has happened; however this is a critical step in being able to recover from grief. Each time you tell someone of about your loss, or simply speak the words "the baby died" it helps to make the loss become real.

Every person is unique and will have a different grief experience. This applies to the acceptance of loss as well. Julia described her experience by saying:

"I felt that if God wanted this child to be born it would be. Besides, I knew that many times a child that was miscarried usually had some type of birth defect. I was actually relieved because I already had three children and was concerned as to how we could afford another child."

If possible, holding the baby can help you accept the loss. Velicia was able to hold her son, and she described the experience:

"I held him... and accepted that this had really happened. I held him and cried when I realized he wasn't sleeping."

After my miscarriage, I opted not to undergo a D&C, but instead to let nature take its course. The experience of my unborn baby leaving my body is still indescribable. It felt like I had a front row seat at a horrible event I never wanted to attend.

As difficult as it was, it did give me the opportunity to actually 'see' my baby. Not the wriggling newborn that I had dreamed of holding, but a small kidney-shaped sac that held my tiny child inside. In the moments I had, I said goodbye and I cried tears that stung with the reality that my baby had died. It was an emotional release for me that helped me to move toward the next phase of my grief.

Kathy described a similar feeling when she recalled her own experience with saying goodbye:

> *"The biggest event was just holding a bear that I pretended was the baby and saying hello and goodbye...It allowed me to share what I would have said, say goodbye and grieve. I cried for 30 minutes, and that was the start of a new day for me."*

A funeral or memorial service for your baby may also help you and your family members to accept the reality that your baby is gone. This can be as formal as a graveside service, or as informal as a simple ceremony for the immediate family

If the loss occurred earlier in the pregnancy, a remembrance ceremony can still be arranged. This will not only validate the baby, it will also help a family in accepting the loss.

Here are some other suggestions to help you in accepting your loss:

- **Share your loss with others**. As difficult as that is, it makes the loss real.
- **Say goodbye.** Hold the baby's sonogram picture, blanket or even a stuffed animal, and say goodbye to your baby. This can be incredibly healing.
- **Have a memorial or remembrance ceremony** for your baby, even if a long time has passed. Chapter 9, *Remembering Your Baby* has some wonderful and simple ideas.

- **Follow your heart** when it is time to put away the baby's things. Wait until you feel ready and ask someone else to help if you are not up to it.

Experiencing the Pain of Grief

There is no way to avoid feeling the pain of grief. There are not short cuts, no secrets to getting around it- you must feel the pain of grief to move through it. Kathy explained:

"I had a total sense of loss, and it was very hard for me to go out and face people."

It is important to allow the feelings of grief to occur. Cry when you need to, feel the sorrow, experience the process. There is no other way to get through it.

It may be tempting to parents to quickly become pregnant again to relieve the pain. This not only masks the pain, it hinders recovery.

I met with a colleague several months after my miscarriage. In talking over dinner, we discovered that we had both suffered pregnancy loss. She shared with me that she had become pregnant again only two months after her miscarriage, and she now had a healthy, young child.

Her eyes filled with tears as we spoke, and her voice was shaking. It was painfully clear that she had not worked through her grief. Although the loss had occurred a few years before, it was still a very fresh wound for her.

There is no timetable for grief. It is important to allow time to fully recover from a miscarriage before getting pregnant again. It may seem like the perfect solution to your grief, however it can suppress the grieving process and prevent recovery.

After my miscarriage, my family often asked me when we were going to try again. They were anxious for us to give it another try, but I just wasn't ready. I did not feel I could build a relationship with a new baby, before handling the emotions I was feeling for my child who died.

Everyone has heard the saying "No pain, no gain." This is particularly true when dealing with grief. Allow yourself to feel the emotions and pain of your loss, so you can move on. Velicia explained her experience by saying:

"In a sense, miscarriage can prompt you to 'sleep' through all the things that normally excited or moved you. In some sense, I retreated from everything and everyone, to assess what had happened and pinpoint my place in the world."

Here are some suggestions to help you experience the pain of grief:

- **Give yourself permission to grieve,** and lean on others when you need too. Allow yourself to feel and express your emotions.
- **Learn about miscarriage and grief,** and read stories about others facing loss. You can visit the local bookstore, library, or even go online. Visit www.HopeXchange.com and see the list of websites in the *Resource* section of this book.
- **Talk with others** facing pregnancy loss, go online, or join a support group. A listing of support groups is included in the *Resource* section of this book.
- **Write!** Writing to heal requires no special skill or talent and it is very therapeutic. Simply begin with "I feel..." Keeping a journal or writing daily can lead you through your grief.

Talking with others and writing are both excellent ways to move toward recovery. Kathy explained that talking with a friend helped her to heal:

"I was very lucky that someone I had worked with also experienced a miscarriage. She called me every day I was home just to talk and share feelings."

Putting your feelings into words can validate them and provide a healthy outlet. Velicia shared with me that writing her thoughts down for this book actually brought her closure and healing years after her pregnancy loss occurred.

Adjusting to a New Life

When a baby dies during pregnancy, or shortly after, the hopes and dreams of the parents die with it. If the couple has no other children, the loss can be even more devastating because the 'family' has died as well.

Pregnancy loss causes a void, and this emptiness must be addressed in order for parents to adjust to a life without their baby. For the woman, the physical connection between mother and child is even greater. She must overcome the feeling that a part of her is gone.

As a couple, the baby that would have started a family or added a new sibling for existing children is gone. There is an adjustment for the parents as well as the children who were expecting a new little brother or sister. This can provide added pressure for parents, as they feel concern about the impact of grief on their remaining children.

At this point you find ways to incorporate the memory of your baby into your existing lives. You will never forget the child who died; you will find ways to remember your baby as an important part of your past. As a couple, or even a family, you will form a new view of your future. Velicia explained:

> *"I had chosen a new life for us and [my baby] Shelby was part of me still."*

An important part of adjusting is resuming the life you had before you experienced the loss. Anna explained:

> *"I remember going back to work pretty quickly. It seemed easier to me to be working and busy than to be at home by myself, dwelling on it."*

Of course your life has been changed, and as a person you have been impacted by the loss, but you learn to return to an altered state of 'normal.' Velicia described it this way:

"You return to being able to take life for granted. Thank God for the 'normalness!'"

Here are some suggestions to help you adjust:

- **Return to work**. Going back to work can help you to feel that you are getting back to your routine. It is also helpful to be surrounded by familiar and caring co-workers.
- **Keep your routine** as normal as possible. Maintaining structure will help you feel a sense of control.
- **Volunteer**. Helping others actually helps to keep your mind off of yourself, and it can improve your perspective. This is both rewarding and healing.
- **Indulge yourself.** Get a message, go shopping, or treat yourself to a facial or manicure. Anything you find relaxing or soothing will help.
- **Recognize your progress**. Notice when you can get through a few hours or days without pain. Find something you are thankful for, laugh, look forward to something. Recognize when you can talk about your baby more easily or feel less preoccupied with yourself and your loss.
- **Get counseling** if you cannot function normally, you feel no relief, or your grief has gone on for too long. If, despite all of your efforts, you cannot cope or adjust, seek professional help.

Readjusting the hopes and dreams you had before your loss is not easy, but it is an important step in moving on with life. It allows you to create a new place for your baby and move on to new hope and new dreams for your future.

Emotionally Relocating Your Baby

Your baby will be a part of you and your memories throughout your life. Moving toward healing means forming a new emotional bond with your child, one that incorporates your baby's memory into your life and allows you to move on.

You will always feel a connection with your child who died; this is normal. Finding ways to continue that bond, while moving towards a new state of 'normal' is an important step in healing and recovery. We will look at several ways to remember your baby in *Chapter 9*.

Expecting a child requires a lot of emotional energy and planning. After a pregnancy loss, that energy is sapped by the grieving process, and the emotions that go with it. During recovery, however, you will move on by rebuilding and reorganizing your life and discovering new ways to direct that energy.

What does that mean? It means that you will use the emotional energy that you were spending on your baby in other activities or relationships. You probably have formed new attachments and new ties with others while dealing with your loss. This can create long lasting relationships that are good places to direct some of that energy.

It is healthy to use your emotional energy in new ways or even strengthen relationships you already have. Becoming closer to your spouse, remaining children, parents, siblings, close friends, or even God can be very rewarding.

Velicia described her experience with family relationships, saying:

> "My mother-in-law passed away and I had to be the strong one. I had to come back into my own life and take care of those who were left, my husband, father and sister-in-law... and my babies that had been 'without' their mother for at least a year."

You can even use some of your energy to invest in yourself. Take care of your health, get into shape, focus on your career, or spend time on a hobby you enjoy.

Here are some suggestions to help you find ways to reinvest:

- **Tell your loved ones and friends how you feel about them** often. Spend time with family and close friends.
- **Make a list of hobbies, activities, and interests** you would like to do again or try for the first time. Follow up on one each month.
- **Help someone else facing loss or grief**. One of the final steps in healing is sharing your experience with others.

It is important to use the emotional energy that you would have given to your baby in new ways. This is a vital step in recovering from grief and moving on with your life.

Hope Returns

Recovering from grief, and accepting your loss and your new life is not easy. But as time progresses you will find that things get a little easier as you go. Eventually your good days will outnumber the bad ones, and slowly hope emerges. Velicia described it by saying:

" Hope doesn't just happen one day. It's the 'noticing' of life's paths in the sand around us, the remembrance of things that tasted good before."

You will never stop missing your baby and there will be times that remind you of your pain. Velicia shared with me that she always 'felt blue' around the same time each year. One day it occurred to her that it was the month that her baby died.

Of course you will always wish that you had your baby. But life does become easier and you learn to laugh again and, yes, even hope again. Eventually you become able to speak of your baby with a sense of peace, and you find yourself planning once again for the future. Kathy explained that:

"I always had hope- never lost that, and perhaps it was because we already had a wonderful son."

Velicia shared her view on hope, saying:

> "Hope emerges everyday,
> Being conscious everyday for my children
> growing and learning,
> The little lines around my eyes that don't
> disappear an hour after I wake up,
> The initial shock of new love, being vulnerable
> enough to say I trust you to love me,
> The cycles of growth over the years,
> This book."

Samuel Smiles' profound words about hope inspired the title of this book:

"Hope is like the sun, which, as we journey toward it, casts the shadow of our burden behind us."

Questions to Ask Yourself

As you move toward acceptance and recovery, consider the following questions:

- **Have I accepted the loss** of my baby? If not, why? Have I said goodbye to my baby?
- **Am I allowing myself to feel the pain** of grief? If not, why?
- **Have I adjusted to life without my baby?** How?
- **Am I moving on** with my life? How?

Have you accepted the loss of your baby? Write about it now:

_____

_____

_____

_____

_____

If the questions you have just answered helped you to identify areas that need focus, decide on two to three actions you will take to address them.

Use this space to write them down:

"Grief drives men into habits of serious reflection, sharpens the understanding and softens the heart."
~ *John Adams*

Chapter 9

Remembering Your Baby

Commemorating the loss of your baby can be a good way to move through the grieving process. For parents, it is a way to remember and reflect on your baby. Even though the child's life was a brief one, it can bring healing and closure for the family.

There are many ways to honor and remember your baby. The choices you make may depend on the circumstances of your loss, but the process will help you to feel close to your baby as you grieve.

Services for the Baby

In some circumstances, a funeral or memorial service may be appropriate. If your baby lived for a brief time, died shortly after birth, or was a stillbirth, you may want to consider a small, public service. Placing the service in your local paper to make others aware is up to you. You must decide what feels right for you and your family.

There is no right or wrong way to conduct a memorial service for your baby. You may wish to have a 'traditional' funeral and hold a graveside or church service. It can be a small public gathering, a private service, or even just immediate family. Your clergy or hospital social worker can help make arrangements.

If your loss occurred earlier in the pregnancy, you may still have a memorial service for your baby. You can hold a service in your church or even in a park or garden. You may invite family and close friends or limit it to your immediate family.

You can ask a pastor or member of clergy to conduct a brief service, or you may choose to simply say a few words. Scatter rose petals, put a message in a baby bottle and toss it out to sea, or release balloons with personal messages inside.

It is never too late to have a service for your baby. If some time has passed, you may select a special date such as the day the baby died, the baby's birthday, or due date.

The important thing is that you and your family have set aside a time to honor and remember your baby. Make decisions that feel right for you.

Naming Your Baby

It may be something you have not thought of, or do not see a need for, but naming your baby can make him or her more real. You will remember the baby for the rest of your life, and it can feel more comfortable to have a name to call your child.

Even if you do not know the sex of your baby, you can select a name that fits either gender. Alex, Sidney, Taylor, and Jesse are examples of names that work for boys and girls. You may have gotten 'a feeling' about the sex of the baby and choose to go with that gender.

If you were planning to 'save the names' you selected for your next baby, you may find that you will change your mind later. Chances are that you will not want to use those names next time- it just may not feel right.

If you have family names such as 'Junior,' then by all means, save that name for your next baby. You can always select a different name for the baby who died.

You may find that your family, or even spouse, does not feel comfortable naming your baby. If that is the case, or if you simply prefer, choose a name yourself and keep it in your heart where your baby is already.

Memorializing Your Baby

There are countless ways to remember and honor your baby. No matter how much time has passed since your miscarriage, it is never too late to memorialize your child.

You can find comfort and healing by incorporating your baby's memory into your life. Here are some suggestions:

- **Create a memory box**. Include any mementos you may have from your baby. A positive pregnancy test, a toy, stuffed animal or outfit you bought for the baby (if you do not have one, then buy one). If you have the baby's ID bracelet, footprints and handprints, or the blanket he or she was wrapped in, include those. Anything you may have that reminds you of your pregnancy or your baby can be included, even if you just have a few things. You may also want to add:
  - A letter to your baby.
  - A birth or name certificate. If you did not receive one, consider making one.
  - A poem or quotation that reminds you of the baby.

  If you do not feel creative enough to design your box, the Memory Box Artist Program can make one for you. Details are listed in the *Resource* section in the back of this book.
- **Make a donation in your baby's name**. Publicly acknowledge your child by making a charitable donation, or give something to a needy child that is the same age your child would have been now. Also consider submitting an article or poem about your baby to a newspaper or magazine.

- **Make something for the baby** such as a quilt, a painting, a cross stitch, an outfit, a piece of pottery or furniture.
- **Buy a piece of jewelry** that symbolizes your baby. Your baby's birthstone, or an engraved necklace with your baby's name can be good choices. See the *Resource* section of this book for information on merchants who offer these items.
- **Plant a tree or garden** in memory of your baby. You may even choose a houseplant or indoor tree. Decorate the tree at special times of the year to remember your baby.
- **Add your baby to the family tree**. If you named your baby, add him or her permanently to the family by including the baby in your family tree.
- **Donate baby items** that you may have bought or received to a worthy charity. You may also do this in your baby's name.
- **Have a celebration** each year on your baby's birthday or due date.
- **Include your baby in the hospital's Remembrance Book.** Most hospitals have a remembrance book, and even if your baby did not die in a hospital, you can contact the Chaplin at your local hospital.
- **Have a photo taken of the baby.** Even if you requested not to see the baby, you may change your mind later. Get a sonogram or photo of the baby and keep it in a safe place.
- **Light a candle** for the baby every evening until you feel you do not need to anymore. After that, burn it once a month or on special anniversaries.
- **Have a star named after your baby.** Information on this can be found in the *Resource* section of this book.
- **Remember your baby online**. There are a number of websites with free memorial sections. See a list in the back of this book.
- **Remember Me Bears** is a website that will make a bear for your baby made from fabric you provide. It could be from baby's blanket or clothing.

Information on this can be found in the *Resource* section.

Remembering your baby is a very personal thing. There is no right or wrong way to honor your child. Taking the time to memorialize your baby will bring you closure and comfort as your move through your grief, and work toward recovery.

Questions to Ask Yourself

Consider the following questions about remembering your baby:

- **Have I had a memorial service for my baby?** If not, why? If so, did it meet the family's needs?
- **Have I named the baby?** If not, why?
- **Do I remember my baby on special days?** When? How? Is the entire family included?
- **Do I have an item that commemorates the baby?** If so, what is it? If not, would I like to have one? What would it be?

Reflect on the memorial service or ceremony you had for your baby. Write about it now:

_____

_____

_____

_____

_____

_____

_____

_____

_____

_____

_____

If the questions you have just answered identified areas that you would like to change or focus on, decide on two to three actions you will take to address them.

Use this space to write them down:

_____

_____

_____

_____

_____

_____

_____

_____

_____

_____

_____

_____

_____

_____

_____

_____

_____

Chapter 10

Handling the Holidays

*H*olidays and special events are normally a time of joy and celebration, however they can become a painful reminder of your loss. Seeing family members, making decisions, and attending the holiday activities you usually enjoy can take on a different outlook after the loss of a child.

If you begin feeling sadness during the holidays or a special occasion, think about why you are feeling that way; process those feelings and accept them. It is a perfectly normal reaction to your grief. Taking this step ahead of time may help you to avoid some uncomfortable moments in public.

Should I Go?

Ask yourself if you are ready to attend family gatherings or parties. This will give you the opportunity to let someone know your decision in advance. Knowing that you would have planned to share your new baby at these celebrations could make them difficult and even tearful for you. Give yourself the option to gracefully bow out of the activity.

Asking yourself these questions before a special event may help:

- **Can I handle this?** Is this something I would enjoy? If so, it could be a good way to lift your spirits.
- **What does my spouse think?** Will it cause problems if I do not attend?
- **Would the holiday or special event be the same if I don't attend?** Deciding not to attend a Christmas play will not take away from the holiday season; however deciding not to attend Thanksgiving dinner will certainly change the Thanksgiving holiday.

Thinking through these questions ahead of time can help you arrive at a decision that is right for you, and one that will not negatively impact your spouse or your family.

Help for the Holidays

The holidays can be a great way to occupy your mind, keep your hands busy, and put you in the company of supportive friends and loved ones. All of these things can be helpful during a time of grief.

However, there will still be times of pain and situations that serve as reminders of your loss. Be sure to take steps to make the holidays as peaceful and joyful as possible.

Here are some suggestions:

- **Set aside private time** for yourself. Shedding a few tears in private can be a great stress reliever and it will reduce your frustration throughout the day.

- **Plan ahead of time**. Make shopping lists, organize your tasks, and leave plenty of time to accomplish them. Reducing some of the normal headaches of the holidays can alleviate added pressures.
- **Educate others on your needs**. If you prefer your family talk about your baby rather than avoid the subject, let them know ahead of time.
- **Do something different**. You may find that changing your holiday routine or allowing someone else to host an event you normally plan can give you a new outlook and reduce stress.
- **Do something for someone else.** Buy a gift for someone in need, adopt a less-fortunate family, or make a donation in your baby's memory. Helping others is a great way to heal.

The holidays should be a time of joy and celebration. Taking some steps to prepare for them, and allowing yourself the space you need, can make them a better experience for you.

Your Children

Holidays and special events are especially important to children. If you have children it is critical to consider their needs during the holidays. Although you may feel like canceling the season all together, your children will need you more than ever during this special time.

When parents are feeling grief, their emotional focus tends to shift inward and away from remaining children. The holidays are a time when your children will want to feel loved and important. Be sure to give them plenty of affection and attention during this time. Otherwise, children can feel that the child who has died is more important than they are. They will need to hear how much you care about them. This reassures them of their place in the family, as well as their place in your heart.

Your children will need to feel joy and celebration during the holidays. Be sure that you do not unknowingly dampen their spirits or their ability to enjoy special events.

Ensure that the holidays continue to be a special time for your children. They will need to feel stability and hope for the family. Taking care of yourself and taking the steps you need to get through the holidays will be important for you and your children.

Mother's Day- Am I a Mother?

Of all of the holidays a woman must face after pregnancy loss, Mother's Day is the hardest. A time that was supposed to be a celebration of a new life and a new motherhood, is instead a time of sadness and grief.

There is nothing that will lessen the pain of your loss on a day set aside to honor mothers; however there are some preparations you can make to ensure the day has meaning for you. Mother's Day can be a time to remember your baby, rather than a dreaded event you must endure every year.

The best gift you can give yourself on Mother's Day is the acknowledgement that you are a mother. You carried a child inside- the very definition and essence of motherhood. You may not have a baby to hold in your arms, but you do have one forever in your heart.

If you feel uncomfortable being recognized as a mother at a banquet or other function, substitute an activity you would feel good about. If you would rather not receive or wear a flower, then wear an item that helps you to connect with your baby, such as a piece of jewelry that includes the baby's birthstone. It is important to let your spouse and family know what you need during this emotional time.

Mother's Day can be a great time for a husband and wife to talk about their baby and what the baby meant to them. Talking about the dreams you shared for your baby and your family can be a great way to strengthen a marriage. Take a walk, have a quiet dinner, or just set aside some time to remember your baby together.

If you have not chosen a name for your baby, Mother's Day can be a good time to select one. Often times Fathers will not be ready to do this, or may not see the need. If so, a mother can name her baby and keep the name in her heart. Choosing a name can be very healing.

Writing a letter to your baby may also be a good way to observe Mother's Day. Putting your thoughts and feelings for your child on paper can also be a good way to heal.

The way you chose to spend Mother's Day should be your decision and one you make ahead of time. Setting time aside to remember and talk about your baby will make you 'feel' more like a mom on the very day designed to do that.

Keep in mind that your spouse may experience similar feelings on Father's Day. Offer the same considerations for him and ask how he would like to spend the day.

Questions to Ask Yourself

Consider the following questions regarding the holidays:

- **Am I thinking through my feelings before holiday events**? Do I allow myself to say no?
- **Am I setting aside private time** for myself?
- **Have I considered the needs of my remaining children during the holidays**? Am I ensuring that their needs are met?
- **Have I thought about how I would like to spend Mother's Day** each year?
- **Have I considered the feelings of my spouse on Father's Day?**

How have you handled the holidays since the loss of your baby? Write about it now:

_____

_____

_____

_____

If the questions you have just answered helped you to identify focus areas, decide on two actions you will take to address them.

Use this space to write them down:

_____

_____

_____

_____

_____

_____

_____

_____

_____

_____

_____

_____

_____

_____

_____

_____

_____

Chapter 11

Dealing With Others

The loss of a child is devastating news for any parent. One of hardest parts of a miscarriage is finding the strength to tell family and friends what has happened.

Pregnancy loss not only affects the parents; it involves family and friends for a long time to come. Loved ones can provide a wonderful support system, offering you comfort and encouragement. On the other hand, dealing with others can also present unique challenges.

Telling Others About the Loss

I remember having to share the news of my miscarriage with my sister. She knew that I was spotting and had gone to the doctor. She just happened to call only minutes after I arrived at home. I had just received the shocking news, and now I would have to speak the words..."we lost the baby." It made it all seem more real- having to speak the words.

Anna recalled:

"I remember the day I got home from the doctor's office, after just learning that there 'wasn't a heartbeat,' and how I dreaded having to call my parents and closest friends. I knew everyone else would hear about it, but I dreaded making those calls. What struck me as odd that day was that the person I dreaded telling the most was my best friend. I wasn't sure why I felt that way."

How do you find the words to tell others, when you can hardly believe the news yourself? There is no right or wrong way- there are no rules to follow. However, simply being straightforward can make the task a little easier. If you feel comfortable, you can even ask family members to help share the news with other family and friends.

If no one knew your were pregnant, you may be tempted to keep the news to yourself. This would take away your family's ability to help and support you. There is no reason to pretend that it is not affecting you, or that your baby was not real. Be sure to tell others- they will want to be there for you.

Some states now issue death certificates for babies who die as a result of a miscarriage. This provides an excellent chance for parents to choose a name for the baby, and be able to tell others the baby's name and the day the baby died. You may even want to use email as a way to notify those outside of your family and closest friends.

Many times fathers may find it easier to notify co-workers, while mothers contact family, the church and close friends. As a couple, you should decide what feels right and make the decisions that are best for you. It is important to share the task of telling others, as it begins the grieving process for both of you.

As difficult as it is, each time you say, "The baby died," it helps you to accept the loss as real. This is an important step in the grief process. As they share the burden of telling others together, a husband and wife can lean on one another and draw closer during a difficult time.

Telling Other Children

Explaining the loss of an expected new brother or sister to a child of any age is hard. While experiencing your own grief, you are also concerned about the reaction of your children and how they will cope with the news.

When I suffered my miscarriage, my stepdaughter was a young teenager. She had been very excited that we were having a baby and I so dreaded telling her. I asked my husband to tell her before she saw me. Something inside me wanted to be sure that she had time to herself to process the news.

The instant I saw her I hugged her tightly and just said, "I'm so sad..." I wanted her to know how much the baby meant to me, but I did not want her to worry that I was falling apart. I still remember feeling that she was holding me up as I hugged her that day.

It is important to be honest and straightforward with children about the loss. Even young children understand more than we often give them credit for. Failing to properly explain what has happened can leave young children feeling anxious or afraid. They may even worry that the same event that caused their new brother or sister to 'go to heaven' could also happen to them.

This is a time that young children will need to feel safe from harm and reassured that you will still have time for them. They may worry that your grieving will leave little time to spend with them. There are some great books that offer advice on telling young children about pregnancy loss, you can find information in the *Resource* section of this book.

Older children may worry about your well-being. They will need to feel assured that you are okay and you will get through the grieving process. It is also important to let them know that as a family, you may face some tough days, but you will all make it through this difficult time.

No One Will Talk About It

Uncomfortable fidgeting, a long silence or a quick change of the subject, are things you may encounter when trying to talk about your loss with family and friends. You will often find that even those closest to you will avoid the topic.

Although your family and friends see you hurting and care about you deeply, they may feel that they do not know how to help, or what to say. Many even believe that avoiding the topic of your baby will help you to forget and move on faster. Nothing could be farther from the truth.

It is perfectly fine to let your family and friends know that you would like to talk about your baby. Often times they may be worried that the slightest mention may have you bursting into tears, and that may happen. However, it is a very important part of the grief process. Be sure to let your family and friends know what you need. They want to be there for you, they just may not know how. Anna said of her family:

> *"They were very thoughtful and considerate. They sort of 'pampered' me in some ways right at the beginning-which was very sweet."*

Kathy explained that her loved ones helped by:

> *"Just being there to talk with, having a listening ear, sharing their sadness with me, reminding me of the wonderful son we had, sharing prayers with me and just being there if I needed something."*

Although families can offer a great deal of support, you may often feel alone because it is difficult to truly understand pregnancy loss if you have not personally experienced it. Remember to seek out others who have shared this experience. Online chat rooms, support groups, and churches can be a great place to meet others dealing with pregnancy loss.

I was stunned at the number of my close friends and acquaintances that had suffered a miscarriage. By bringing up the topic, it gave them the opportunity to share their own stories with me. In fact, the stories and quotations you see throughout this book are in fact those very women- my close friends, who opened their hearts to me.

Help Others Help You

People who care about you will most likely feel grateful to know how they can help. Many times, they just aren't sure how to act or what to say. This can leave you feeling more alone and even angry.

Remember that there are people around you that want to help; however you may have to give them a little guidance on how to do that.

Here are some suggestions:

- **Let them know** that phone calls, visits and even just listening are very important and helpful to you.
- **Tell them that it is okay to ask you questions** about what happened. Let them know that it helps for you to talk and even cry about it.
- **Suggest that family members offer to do specific things** for you like watching your children or dropping off the dry cleaning, rather then just saying, "Call me if you need me."
- **Ask them to remember the baby**. If you named your baby, ask them to use your baby's name. Let them know that you will not forget your baby, even if you have or will have other children.
- **Thank them** for their concern and support and let them know how much you appreciate them.

Over time you may notice that people's concern and support seem to dwindle. That does not mean they no longer care, they may assume that you no longer need it. Grief is a very individual process, so be sure to let those around you know what you need.

Dealing with People

Many times people have no idea what to say or how to comfort someone who has suffered loss. Our culture fails to address mourning and grief, and as a result people can actually say things that are hurtful, rather than helpful. Anna realized this and commented:

"I know that people don't always know WHAT to say. So sometimes they try, and just say the wrong thing."

Dealing with insensitive comments can be difficult. Although the person's intentions are most likely good, it can be uncomfortable responding to them. Here are some common comments to loss, followed by some suggested replies:

- "I'm sure it was for the best."
I don't really feel that way. I would feel best if I had my baby.

- "At least you weren't farther along..."
I think a baby is still a baby- even if it's a small one.

- "You'll see your baby in heaven."
I would have liked to see my baby here on earth.

- "Well, you can just have another."
Yes, but a new baby won't replace the child that died.

You may find the easiest way to deal with difficult people is simply to avoid them. If the person is a relative such as a mother-in-law (and often it is), ask your husband to take her calls and stay busy during visits.

Remember, most people are not intending to be hurtful, so try not to take their comments to heart. If you find that someone is truly upsetting you, simply avoid that person until you are ready to deal with him/her.

How Many Children Do You Have?

How many children do you have? It seems like a simple question, but for parents who have suffered pregnancy loss, it can be a very difficult one to answer.

Only a handful of states legally recognize miscarriage as the "death of a child." Society does not generally consider a baby who dies due to miscarriage as a child to be counted. As terrible as that sounds, in most cases, it will be up to you to decide.

It is most important that you feel comfortable with the decision you make. You might find it comforting to include the child who died as a part of your family. On the other hand, you may feel that it brings up a topic you do not wish to share with a complete stranger. It is your call.

I find that I often answer that question differently in different situations. If I meet someone I am comfortable with, and the setting is appropriate, I may mention that, "I also lost a baby," in answering how many children I have. Most times, the person says, "I'm sorry to hear that," and the conversation moves on.

It makes me feel good to recognize and remember the child I never knew. I do not feel compelled to do that in every circumstance, however when I feel the need, I follow my heart.

Only you can decide what is right for you. Do not feel that you cannot count your child who died if you would like to do that. It can be a good way to validate your baby and help in the grieving process.

You may occasionally find that dealing with others presents unique challenges, but remember how much love and support you will gain from caring family and friends. It is up to you to show them how to best help you and you can all reap the rewards.

Questions to Ask Yourself

Consider the following questions about others:
- **Have I told family and friends how to best help me?** When? How?

- **Have I sought others who have experienced a miscarriage?** Who? How?
- **Have I been straightforward in explaining the loss to remaining children?**
- **How will I answer when people ask me how many children I have?**

If these questions have identified focus areas, decide on two actions you will take to address them.

Use this space to write them down:

_____

_____

_____

_____

_____

_____

_____

_____

_____

_____

_____

_____

_____

_____

_____

_____

Chapter 12

Families and Grief

℘regnancy loss causes pain that affects the entire family. Each of you will feel grief in an individual and unique way because grief is a person's internal reaction. However, you will experience mourning together since mourning is the external expression of grief.

A loss often affects family members as individuals and together as a unit. The differing grief that each one experiences and the various ways that each one expresses it can be complex and even painful. One person may feel intense grief and express strong emotions, while another feels compelled to appear 'strong' and chooses not to mourn.

Marriages can also bend and even break under the strain of loss and mourning. Men and women often grieve differently, and they may feel too overwhelmed to reach out to one another. We will discuss this in detail in the next chapter, *Grief and Your Marriage.* Nontraditional or blended families can face additional challenges as they move through the mourning process. They may not have the typical family structure that allows them to understand and support one another consistently. They may also be denied legal protections that are available to other families. In addition, extended family members may fail to understand or recognize their grief.

Men, Women & Children Grieve Differently

Each family member will feel and express grief in a completely unique way. The failure to accept these differences can cause additional stress and even conflict between family members. During a time when a family needs one another most, the individual pain of grief can drive them apart.

Men

When facing loss, men generally put their feelings into action. They often experience their pain physically rather than emotionally. A man may tend to focus on goal-oriented tasks that require thinking and action. For this reason, he may put his efforts into planting a memorial garden or writing a eulogy.

In other cultures, men have been noted as using rituals to relieve the pain of anger or grief. Physical ceremonies such as shooting bows and arrows have been observed as outlets for grief and sorrow.

Activity can give men a sense of control and accomplishment as they experience grief. Even if he decides to share details of his loss with friends, it may likely be during shared activities such as fishing or sporting events.

Men will often react to the stress of grief by exhibiting behavior that scientist refer to as "fight-or-flight." This type of reaction means that individuals who are confronted with stress will either react aggressively ("fight"), or withdraw or flee from the situation ("flight").

A man will often allow himself to cry during grief, but he will usually do so alone, or even in the dark. This may lead other family members to believe that he is not grieving at all.

Women

In general, our society teaches women that it is acceptable for them to be open with their feelings. They will often feel a greater need to talk with others and share their emotions with supportive friends and family members.

In many cases, women seek non-judgmental listeners who are comfortable with a show of emotion. This provides them with an outlet for the grief they are feeling.

Women often respond to the stress of grief with a reaction called "tend-and-befriend." This means that they may feel compelled to protect or nurture their children or others ("tend") and seek out social contact and support from others ("befriend"). For this reason, women may have the desire to join a support group, while men, on the other hand, generally do not.

Even with our society's ability to accept strong emotions and feelings from women, it is typical for our culture to criticize them as they deal with grief. All too often, women are said to be too sentimental or even 'weak' when they are seen expressing the painful emotions of grief. This causes some women to feel the need to suppress their feelings, or believe that they are failing to be 'strong.' However, it is often found that women are experiencing the grief- feeling the pain, while others around may be avoiding grief work.

Children

Children feel grief as deeply and uniquely as adults, however they express it differently than the grownups around them. A child's reaction will largely depend on their intellectual capacity and emotional development at the time of the loss.

In many cases, children often understand much more than adults realize. During times of grief and loss, it is critical to share honest and simple facts with children.

They need accurate information and the freedom to ask questions as they process their grief.

As children grieve they will require the need to express their feelings and receive consistent and stable attention from family members, especially parents. They may not be able to express their feelings right away, so keep in mind that an apparent lack of reaction from a child who has received news of a loss does not mean that he or she does not understand. However, it may take time for the child to be able to process and deal with the loss. We will talk in more detail about children in Chapter 14, *Children and Grief.*

Grandparents

Families should be aware of the double grief that grandparents face during pregnancy loss. They not only feel the pain and grief of their own children, but they also experience the loss of a grandchild.

Grandparents can be left feeling helpless, unable to remove the pain and sorrow their child is feeling. They may feel uncertain of how to offer support or they may find that listening or hearing about the loss is too painful.

Pregnancy loss often leaves grandparents feeling angry or cheated of a joy they may have greatly anticipated. If there are no other grandchildren, the loss can be especially difficult.

How Personalities Affect Grief

Men, women and children will feel grief differently, and their individual personalities will also affect how each one will react to grief and mourning. Each of us has the ability to think and feel, but research shows that people often prefer one type or pattern of reaction over another.

Thinkers

Thinkers often experience and refer to their grief physically and intellectually. It is common for a thinker to seek out information, analyze available facts in order to make an informed decision, and then take action to solve problems. Men commonly fall into this personality pattern, but women can also respond as thinkers.

When facing powerful emotions, thinkers tend to remain detached and strong. They often speak of their grief in very intellectual terms and attempt to remain dispassionate about their feelings. This behavior often causes others to assume that a thinker is cold or has no feelings at all.

Feelers

Feelers generally experience a wide range of emotions when encountering grief and loss. They tend to be very comfortable with showing strong emotions and tears. For this reason they are normally very sensitive to their own feelings, as well as the feelings of others. Women commonly react in this personality pattern, although men can also respond as feelers.

Because feelers experience such intense emotions, it is often difficult for them to rationalize and intellectualize the pain their grief is causing. For this reason, they can appear to be overwhelmed or devastated by a loss.

Suppressors

Suppressors may experience intense grief and have very strong feelings, but they find themselves unwilling or unable to express them. These repressed feelings often drive these individuals to drugs or alcohol in an attempt to numb the pain. Suppressors also find that they are able to let go of their emotions when the influence of drugs or alcohol removes their inhibitions.

No matter what gender or personality patterns exist, grief and mourning are difficult tasks for every family member. Each person must work through feelings of grief so healing and resolution can begin.

Help For Families

Grief is a family affair. It is important that families allow one another the freedom and support they need to move through and beyond their loss. Here are some suggestions for families:

- **Talk about grief and feelings with one another and as a family.** Confront any questions or concerns that surface about how family members are handling their grief.
- **Encourage open discussions** about the loss and do not be afraid to cry together.
- **Accept help and support from others**. Also be sure to recognize when other family members may need additional help.
- **Allow space** for individuals to experience grief in his or her own way without criticism.
- **Try to stick with family routines** as much as possible to foster stability and consistency
- **Individual time**. Allow family members to ask for time alone when it is needed.
- **Remember that everyone in your family will move through grief at a different pace**. Allow time for family members who need it, while enjoying the success of those who are resolving their grief.

Recognizing the differences each of you face in dealing with grief will allow you to pull together during a time when it is most important. Although mourning is difficult, it can make petty conflicts seem less important and help you to grow stronger as a family. Velicia summed it up well when she said:

"Miscarriages happen to families no matter if they understand or not, whether they remain intact or not...Healing is important so you can be able to love those that are still here."

Questions to Ask Yourself

Here are some questions to consider about your family:

- **Have I allowed each of my family members to grieve in their own way?** If not, why?
- **Are we talking openly about our loss?** If not, why?
- **Have I helped to foster a stable family environment?** How?
- **Do I need to ask for help for our family or a family member?** If so, what help do we need?

If these questions have identified focus areas for you and your family, decide on two to three actions you will take to address them.

Use this space to write them down:

_____

_____

_____

_____

_____

_____

_____

_____

_____

_____

_____

_____

_____

_____

"Grief can't be shared. Everyone carries it alone, his own burden, his own way."
~ *Anne Morrow Lindbergh*

Chapter 13

Grief and Your Marriage

*D*uring a time when you and your spouse need each other most, grief can bring an enormous strain to your relationship and even your marriage. The need to lean on one another can be overwhelming when you are buckling under the weight of loss.

It is often said that the death of a child can bring devastation and even divorce to married couples. It will be more important than ever to protect and support the most critical relationship of marriage. This will take effort and understanding from both of you, but it is well worth the work.

Many of the difficulties for couples working through loss, are often the drastic differences in the ways men and woman express and cope with grief. Lack of communication and misunderstandings caused by these differences can be the primary factor in marriage problems that stem from loss. It is crucial to truly listen and seek to understand your mate during this time.

A Mother's Grief

A mother forms a physical bond with an unborn child that cannot be fully understood by any father. The act of 'carrying' a child creates a relationship and attachment with the baby that men are unable to experience. This greatly changes the landscape of grief for mothers who suffer miscarriage. Women feel a physical and emotional emptiness that is unique to a mother.

Women also face the physical effects of a miscarriage. There are hormonal changes and physical pain that must be endured as the body suddenly plummets from a state of pregnancy to a state of non-pregnancy. These physical symptoms can be severe, confusing, and at times even frightening for a woman enduring a miscarriage.

The swift and sudden changes a mother's body faces after a pregnancy loss can be painful and isolating. It can be extremely difficult for women to share the personal details with anyone- even their husbands. This can leave them feeling even more lonely and overwhelmed. Though the physical symptoms of a miscarriage usually end in 4-6 weeks, it can take months for a woman to accept and begin to deal with the loss.

The physical changes that women undergo can sometimes affect sexual desire. It can also be difficult for mothers to resume normal activity when it may serve as a painful reminder of the loss. It may take several weeks for a woman to feel emotionally and physically ready to resume a sexual relationship with her husband.

Mothers often feel an intense need to talk about their baby and the emotions they are feeling. They may seek information on loss and grief and even reach out to others through support groups, especially if they are unable to find family or friends who can listen without judging their feelings.

The experiences of men and women vary greatly during pregnancy loss. It takes the understanding and communication of both partners to work through this difficult time.

A Father's Grief

Fathers can sometimes be forgotten during the grief of miscarriage. Although society expects a woman to show emotion and sorrow, it often expects a man to be the 'strong one' and protector of the family. This can lead to great frustration and lack of support for fathers.

Fathers may find it hard to talk about their loss. Men can have difficulty in expressing their emotions even in the heart of grief. To others, it can appear that fathers are unaffected by the pain of miscarriage, and this could not be farther from the truth. A man's difficulty in putting his feelings into words can cause even his wife to question or doubt the depth of his grief.

Males also experience grief in a more internal and logical way then their female partners. They may handle their emotions through physical activity, work or hobbies. Again, this gives the impression that they have returned to normal routines with little or no impact.

Our culture often leaves us wondering just how to relate to a man facing grief. In many cases, friends and associates will ask, "How is your wife doing?" rather than tread on the shaky ground of male emotions. This can lead to anger and resentment for fathers who can feel a lack of support. They may even begin to feel anger toward their wives who are receiving the attention they crave, but dare not ask for.

Men and women face a very different grief process. These differences can leave each one feeling alone and frustrated. It is critical that husbands and wives work together as a couple, but still allow the space that is needed to grieve as individuals.

Helping Your Husband

You may find yourself feeling confused or even doubting that your husband is experiencing the pain of pregnancy loss. Anna said:

"I did feel angry with my husband afterwards. I didn't feel like it impacted him the way it did me. I felt more 'grown up' and somehow more 'serious' in some odd way. I think I wanted him to feel the same impact- or at least understand it."

It is critical for your marriage and the well-being of your spouse that you work to understand how men and women grieve differently. The life experiences you have each had, along with cultural and personality differences mean that you are going to have separate, *but equal* dealings with grief.

If the lines of communication and support break down during loss, you will find your husband feeling alone and unsupported. It is crucial that you work together to prevent your grief from separating you.

Here are some ways to help your spouse during grief:

- **Give your husband space and freedom to grieve in his own way**. Do not discredit his feelings or judge the actions your husband takes to deal with his grief. Activities, work and hobbies may be his way of working through the pain.
- **Help your husband understand the physical aspects of a miscarriage** and the changes that occur afterwards.
- **Ask for your husband's patience if you are not ready to resume a physical relationship.** Keep in mind that a physical relationship reassures a man that he is loved and needed. Get back to normal as soon as possible.
- **Remember that men normally grieve in private- not in public**. You may not see outward signs that your husband is grieving, but do not be fooled. Understand that a man in grief will find himself in a difficult position- he will be shamed if he expresses deep emotions in public and he will be shamed if he does not.
- **Be aware that men often experience anger differently then women during grief**. While women may tend to point anger inward, men often direct their anger outward. This can manifest as

anger toward you or even God. Remember that
expressed anger is a normal and healthy response,
however hostile behavior is not.

- **Listen.** Remember that some men want to talk,
  but they feel there is no one to listen. A man may
  also be uncomfortable putting his feelings into
  words. Encourage him by listening during those
  times when he does talk about it.
- **Ask what you can do**. It is very important to ask
  your husband what you can do to be of service to
  him during his grief, and then do your best to meet
  his needs.
- **Keep an open mind**. Remember that grief is an
  individual experience. Assuming that a man is not
  feeling pain if he grieves differently than you will
  only cause strife and misunderstanding.

Dealing with pregnancy loss will be difficult for you
and your husband. Understanding one another and giving
the space and support you each need will be critical.

Helping Your Wife

A miscarriage is an intense physical and emotional loss
for a woman. It can be a devastating time of sorrow and
pain that may be difficult for you to fully understand.

It will be critical during this time to be sensitive to the
differences you both will face as you deal with pregnancy
loss. You and your wife will need each other more than
ever, and yet you will need to work through the grief as a
couple and as individuals.

You may be frustrated that you cannot take away the
pain your wife is feeling. You may also feel that her grief is
overtaking her, and she should be feeling better or moving
on.

After my miscarriage, I was worried that my husband
would think I was weak if he knew how I was feeling.
Although he was completely supportive and a tremendous
comfort to me, he occasionally made comments about
"getting back on the horse." I knew he was right, but I was
still feeling the pain of the loss. Then I worried that the

grief I was still experiencing would make me appear weak to him, and I did not want that. As I result, I sometimes stayed silent rather than run the risk of sharing my true emotions.

It is crucial that you work to understand the different grief experiences you will both have, and offer support to your wife without judging her emotions.

Here are some suggestions for helping your wife through this difficult time:

- **Let her cry.** Realize that women are more open with their feelings and find a good cry to be a release of emotion. Be aware that crying is healthy for both men and women, and it can bring much needed relief to those suffering grief.

- **Ask her how she is feeling.** Be aware that the physical aspects of a miscarriage are weighing on your wife. Take an interest in her health and physical recovery.

- **Be patient.** Understand that some women may have difficulty resuming a sexual relationship. Hormones, physical changes and the possibility of getting pregnant can delay sexual desire for women.

- **Allow her to talk about it.** Remember that she will need to verbalize how she is feeling. Be patient and listen. Remind yourself that she does not expect you to offer solutions for the emotions she is feeling, she simply needs a listening ear that will not judge.

- **Realize that your wife will grieve in public.** She may reach out to others or even join a support group. If you do not share her desire to attend, that is fine, but do allow her the space to meet her needs. Keep in mind that attending one meeting with her could allow you to hear how she is feeling in a safe environment. This can be a valuable insight for husbands.

- **Allow her the time she needs to recover.** Resist the urge to tell your wife that she is weak, or taking too long to bounce back.

Realize that men and women often move at a different pace when dealing with pregnancy loss.

- **Do not push too quickly to try again.** Remember that your wife may not be able to think about getting pregnant again for quite some time. The idea can be too much for her to handle while still dealing with the miscarriage.

Getting through pregnancy loss will be difficult for you and your wife. Giving each other the support and understanding you both need will make the journey a little easier.

Trial By Fire- Grief as a Couple

You will often hear that grief and loss bring couples together, but it can actually do just the opposite. The differences in the way you grieve can leave you both feeling alone and misunderstood. It can also be very difficult to support one another when you both feel wiped out by the pain of grief.

Facing grief as a couple can place a strain on you as individuals as well as on your marriage. As your grief leads you in different directions, you may feel disconnected from one another. Problems that already existed in a marriage can become magnified during this emotionally charged time. Velicia described her experience:

> *"Our marriage was unsteady so I knew deep down that although I hoped for us to grieve and grow well together, it wasn't going to happen. ...We had been married for 10 years when I left for good. I don't think we ever recovered."*

While the pain of grief can highlight weaknesses that were present in a marriage, it can also bring a couple together. Making it through a loss together can give a husband and wife the unshakable confidence of knowing that they can make it through anything. It can strengthen the relationship in ways you would not have imagined.

The emotional support my husband offered me after our loss showed a side of him I had not seen; and it was one I greatly needed and appreciated. The experience confirmed what we already knew- we could get through anything together.

It is possible to emerge on the other side of grief with a closer marriage, but it does take work. Facing loss together and thriving as a couple will have to be a priority for you both.

Here are some steps you can take to help your marriage survive the stress of loss:

- **Give each other the freedom to grieve in an individual way.** There are significant differences in the way that men and women handle grief. Some studies conclude that our physical differences may even affect how we choose to grieve. Resist the temptation to feel that your way is the only way to handle loss.
- **Remember the good times.** Think about activities you enjoy as a couple and make time to do them. It can be difficult to plan time to 'have fun' when you are grieving, but it is important to allow yourselves to step away from your sorrow and enjoy one another.
- **Expect tough times.** Be tolerant with your mate and understand that you are both going to fail each other during this turbulent time.
- **Do not lash out at one another**. A woman may be more inclined to verbally attack her spouse during grief, while a man often directs his anger at those around him. In a weakened state of grief, this will only push you apart.
- **Prepare for change.** Loss and grief change people and it will change the face of your marriage. Decide together that this trial will bring you closer and commit to your relationship.
- **Reach out.** Resist the urge to spend time away from your mate or reach out to others who better understand your grief. It is critical to keep the

lines of communication open, and failing to spend time together will only push you apart.

- **Avoid placing blame.** Tossing accusations at your spouse will only place a wedge in your relationship. Understand that feelings of guilt, anger, and confusion are normal during this time. Verbal assaults will leave you both feeling more angry and alone.

- **Love each other.** Be sure to offer the hugs, cuddling, and even physical love that each partner needs to feel secure and supported. Meeting each other's needs for love will bring you closer together and help to heal your grief

- **Seek information and support.** Educate yourselves on grief and try to understand one another. If you are having difficulties resolving your grief as a couple and you feel your marriage is in trouble, get help immediately! A pastor, marriage counselor, or support group can offer the assistance you need. Do not wait until it is too late to seek help.

There are no easy answers for couples dealing with pregnancy loss. It is crucial that you make the decision to put your marriage first and then do it!

Working through grief is never easy, but taking careful steps to support one another can leave you with a more caring and stable marriage. Make the effort required for you and your marriage to grow.

Questions to Ask Yourselves

As you and your spouse work through your grief together, here are some questions to consider as you focus on your marriage:

- **Have we made our marriage a priority?** If not, what actions do we need to take to make the commitment needed?

- **What is the most difficult aspect of grief I am facing now? What is most difficult for my spouse?**
- **How can I better support my spouse?** Each of you should individually consider this question.
- **What is the biggest roadblock** our marriage is facing? What can we do to overcome it?
- **What are some things we enjoy doing as a couple?** When is the last time we have done them? How can we make time for one another?

You may consider answering these questions together, as a couple, if you feel comfortable. Even writing down the answers for yourself can give you a feeling of control over the strain that grief can place on a marriage.

If you have identified focus areas for your marriage, determine at least three things you can do immediately to begin addressing them.

Use this space to write them down:

_____

_____

_____

_____

_____

_____

_____

_____

_____

_____

_____

_____

_____

Use this space for your spouse to write:

_____

_____

_____

_____

_____

_____

_____

_____

_____

_____

_____

_____

_____

_____

_____

_____

"Children suffer not (I think) less than their elders,
but differently."
~ C.S. Lewis

Chapter 14

Children and Grief

*C*hildren can often be forgotten during a time of loss and mourning. Whether you have surviving children of your own, or young family members such as nieces and nephews, pregnancy loss effects children as much as adults.

Allowing children to grieve individually as well as with the family, is critical in helping them to come to terms with the loss. Remember that they may often feel many of the same feelings and emotions that you are facing in your own grief. Although children may not fully understand the event, emotionally they face many of the reactions that grief imposes on adults.

Children's Reactions to Loss

In Chapter 9, *Dealing With Others*, we discussed ways to share pregnancy loss with children. You will remember that honesty and openness were key in telling children about your miscarriage.

A child may appear to be unaffected after hearing of the loss, but that is typically not the case. In fact, young children who continue with an activity or suddenly go out to play are actually attempting to shield themselves from the news because it is too difficult to respond at the time.

Children often respond to loss in small amounts over time. Taking on the full force of grief would be too difficult for a child who has not learned the coping skills and mechanisms that adults count on. For this reason, they may feel many of the same emotions that adults face, but in other ways their experience with loss can be very different.

The ways in which children respond to death and loss varies with their age, past experiences, and their relationship with their parents and other family members. It is important to remember that their grief experience will be personal and individual- just like adults. There will not be a predictable pattern to their behavior.

A grieving child may seem angry one day and the next day he may feel sad. Children may feel loneliness, guilt, fear, and disorganization after suffering a loss. They may 'act out' or seem withdrawn. These are all normal responses to loss, and they will not fall into a structure or predictable pattern.

Children who experience the loss of a future brother or sister may also feel guilt or relief. They could have been worried about sharing attention after the new baby arrived. They may feel fear that they too could die. These children may also feel confused, wondering if they are really a brother or sister to the baby who has died. All of these reactions are normal.

Answering Children's Questions

As children allow themselves to feel the pain of grief in small amounts, they begin to process what has happened. Accepting and coping with the baby's death will bring on more questions and conversations about the loss. It is not unusual for children to go for a period of time without mentioning the loss at all, and then suddenly bombard you with questions. This is perfectly normal and a good sign that the child is beginning to process the loss.

It is critical that you answer children's questions about loss and death as honestly and directly as possible. With young children, avoid using terms such as the baby 'passed away,' or he's gone away. This can cause confusion or even anxiety for a small child who may believe that the baby could possibly return. The child may even wonder if the same thing could happen again- to himself or another sibling.

With children who have no experience with death, you will need to use the words 'death' or 'died' and explain what they mean. Be sure to offer a concrete explanation like the baby cannot hear, breathe, eat, or cry anymore, and he will never be able to. Offer truthful and simple information that does not overload the child.

If you know why the baby died, share that information with children in terms they can understand. If you are unsure, it is fine to share that too. Be sure to let children know that this sort of thing sometimes happens, but usually it does not.

Children may ask questions about the loss that may seem odd or unrelated. Keep in mind that a child's mind does not function in the same way as an adult, and answer the questions as clearly and honestly as you can.

You may also notice that children ask the same questions repeatedly. This is completely natural. Children may not fully understand the answers to their questions the first time they ask. Asking again gives them a chance to understand more each time they ask.

As children grow older, the loss will take on new meaning, prompting more mature questions. Velicia described how her 13 year-old son, Dillan, began asking questions about his brother, who was stillborn when Dillan was only 5 months old:

" When we had a discussion about Shelby [his brother], he said, 'I had a brother? He had a name? What was it?'

Many days later, Dillan was feeling lonely and he came to me and said, 'You know, Mom, I had a brother and we could have been playing together.'

Prompted by this comment were even more questions about what he looked like...which seemed to comfort Dillan."

It is critical that children's questions be treated with honesty and respect by the adults around them. This validates their feelings and allows them to move through the grief process.

What Do You Say to Surviving Children?

Parents who have children and then suffer pregnancy loss have the double sorrow of confronting their own grief while supporting their surviving children as well. This can be especially stressful on a family during a time when you as a parent must be 'strong' for your remaining children.

It can be difficult to convey your own emotions to your children without causing worry over the fate of the family, or even your own well-being. However, it is important that your remaining children understand your feelings because that actually helps to validate their own emotions.

When I was faced with seeing my teenage stepdaughter for the first time after my pregnancy loss, I felt compelled to share with her my feelings of intense sadness. She had been looking forward to a new brother or sister as well, and I needed to let her know that we were all feeling the effects of the loss.

Here are some things you can say to your children:

- "Now that our baby has died, we need you more than ever..."
- " It's important for me (and for you) to talk about the baby whenever we need to..."
- "We don't really know why the baby died and that makes it even harder..."
- "It's hard because we never got to know the baby..."

It is important that your surviving children understand that you have been impacted by the loss, and so have they, but you will all be okay. Children of any age will need reassurance that the family will thrive and have hope and happiness again.

Helping Grieving Children

Acknowledging that children experience the grief and pain of pregnancy loss is the first important step in helping them recover. Allowing children to ask questions, speak honestly about their feelings, and feel safe in their environment is critical for them.

Here are some ways you can help grieving children:

- **Listen!** Let children know that you are there to hear them out without judging. Do not try to anticipate what they are feeling or why- let them tell you. Explain that you want to understand what they are feeling.
- **Include children in planning a memorial.** Make your baby's memorial a family event and be sure to include children in the details. Do not force a child to participate in an event he/she is uncomfortable with, and offer choices when possible. This shows children that they are valued members of the family. Refer back to Chapter 9, *Remembering Your Baby,* for some ideas your children can participate in.
- **Allow children to choose a keepsake.** Help children to select an item that reminds them of the baby. This could be an item that you have already purchased, or one you and the children buy together. This helps to provide a link to the baby.
- **Encourage children to ask questions and share their feelings**. Be patient with younger children's questions and prompt them to share their emotions. Conversations, drawing pictures and even playing games can be a good way for children to share feelings. See the *Resource* section in the back of this book for more.

- **Initiate conversations** with older children and let them know that it may be painful, but it is good to talk about the baby.
- **Be aware of anniversary dates and birthdays**. Children may remember the day the baby died or the baby's due date- the expected birthday. Be sensitive to their needs during these times, as children often experience 're-grief' during those times.
- **Look for physical signs.** Understand that children are physical in their grief. Be aware of their body language and play activities and be nearby to reassure them when needed.
- **Be prepared for grief to return.** As children age, the loss takes on a new and more mature meaning. Expect children to take a long time to recover from the initial impacts of grief and realize that throughout childhood and teen years grief will revisit. Be there to listen when your child needs you.
- **Know when to ask for help.** If you are feeling overwhelmed in your own grief, ask others to assist by spending time with your grieving children. If any symptoms of grief, such as depression, persist in your children seek professional help.

The loss of a baby is a difficult time for parents as well as children. Giving children the love, care and secure environment they need to process their emotions will ensure that they too can face their grief and move toward healing.

Questions to Ask Yourself

If you have suffered a miscarriage and you are caring for remaining children, here are some questions to consider:

- **Am I spending time with my children?** Have I been able to listen and show them that I love and care about them?

- **Do I need to ask for help?** Remember that it is okay and perfectly normal to feel overwhelmed. Just be sure to ask for help for your children if you need it.

If these questions have identified focus areas in how you are dealing with your children, decide on two to three actions you will take to address them.

Use this space to write them down:

_____

_____

_____

_____

_____

_____

_____

_____

_____

_____

_____

_____

_____

_____

_____

_____

_____

_____

_____

_____

_____

"To grieve alone is to suffer most."
~ Talmud

Chapter 15

How Can I Help?
A Resource for Friends & Loved Ones

Note: This chapter is designed to aid the friends and loved ones of grieving parents. As a grieving parent, you may also find the information to be helpful as you talk with others about how to best comfort you.

*F*acing a loss due to miscarriage can have a devastating effect on a couple. For friends and family members of the parents, it can be extremely difficult to know what to say or how to help.

From the moment a woman discovers that she is pregnant, a connection begins for the mother and father. They begin to plan, hope, and dream about the child that will start, or add to, their family. In a society that fails to treat miscarriage as the death of a baby, parents are left isolated and struggling to grieve the loss of their child.

During this time, grieving parents will need you now more than ever. Surrounded by a culture that has not accepted death and loss, a mother and father will often be treated as if the miscarriage was "no big deal." This cannot be further from the truth. Your concern, caring, and support will be vital for them as they deal with the loss.

It is not uncommon to feel helpless, frustrated, or even angry that your loved ones have experienced this terrible pain. You may feel cheated, and most likely you are facing grief of your own. You may even be trying to avoid the loss altogether. These are all normal responses to grief and loss.

It is important to remember that grief is an individual experience. Everyone will feel it differently based on culture, past history, and life experiences. Being available to listen and offer support without judging is critical.

What Should I Say?

Knowing what to say to someone in the depths of grief can be very difficult. If you have never experienced a similar loss, it can be even harder to decide what would be helpful.

I still think about my twin sister's reaction when I had to tell her about my miscarriage. I had not told anyone yet...my voice wavered, and the tears ran down my face as I told her "we lost the baby."

After a long pause my sister began to speak, and I could hear that she was holding back tears. She said, "I couldn't even begin to imagine what you are going through right now..."

After having three healthy children, she really could not imagine the pain of a miscarriage, and hearing her say that was so comforting to me. Even the emotion she expressed validated my own sorrow. Her response was exactly what I needed.

Comforting someone in grief is never easy, but there are some things you can say that will help.

Things to Say

- "I am so sorry about your loss."
- "This must be so hard for you..."
- "I can't even imagine how you must feel right now..."
- "I am so sad for you...please tell me what happened..."
- "How are you doing with all of this...?
- "I am here for you if you want to talk about it..."
- "I'm here to listen anytime..."
- "Please tell me what I can do to help..."
- "How are you feeling...?"
- "Can I bring over dinner...?"

Things to Avoid

- "It was God's will..."
- "I'm sure it was for the best, the baby was probably deformed..."
- "You can always have another one..."
- "At least you weren't farther along..."
- "I know how you must feel..."
- "Maybe you should have...."
- "At least you'll see the baby in heaven someday..."
- "You'll get over it..."
- "You wouldn't have wanted the baby to be born with something wrong..."

It can feel awkward and even difficult to find the right words to say to a grieving couple, but it is an important way to support them. Parents dealing with loss need to talk about their baby and how they are feeling. Even just admitting that you do not know what to say is comforting to them.

What Can I Do to Help?

Even when close family members are facing loss, it can be tough to decide what to do. Just knowing that you are around to offer love and support will help. Velicia said of her family:

> *"My mother and grandmother were helpful, as my mom had lost two...They were just there for me, open, talking and two silent supporters of my return to the land of the living."*

Kathy said her friends and family helped by:

> *"Just being there to talk with, having a listening ear, sharing their sadness with me, reminding me of the wonderful son we had, sharing prayers with me and just being there if I needed something."*

On the other hand, some women find very little help from family members. Julia described her experience with her family:

> *"Except for my mother; family, friends, nor husband contributed to the healing process."*

I received a package in the mail a few days after my pregnancy loss. A few close friends sent me a beautiful gift along with a card and a book of encouraging scriptures. It was very comforting to know that they had done such a thoughtful and caring thing for me. Anna described a similar experience saying:

> *" I remember receiving a card from a cousin who lived across the country, not someone that I spoke with very often. She explained that she had gone through a similar circumstance. It was so thoughtful of her, and I was very touched at how people were so willing to reach out."*

Remember that you may be dealing with your own grief- especially if the couple is a part of your family. This means that you may be working through your pain, while offering support to your loved ones. Keep in mind that your grief experiences will be different.

It is critical that you do not judge the couple's feelings and emotions. Grief impacts everyone individually, so listening in a way that does not discredit any feelings is vital.

Here are some ways you can help:

- **Listen.** Above all, grieving parents need to express their emotions, talk about their baby, and reflect on their loss. Offering to hear without judging is one of the most helpful things you can do. Try to let the parents do the talking. Remember that silence is okay, so be careful not to engage in too much small talk or idle chatting.

- **Keep in touch**. Resist the urge to avoid the couple and their pain. Knowing that you care is important to them. Be sure to ask them how they are doing. Avoiding the subject does not help in fact, it leads to more pain and frustration for parents.

- **Remember Dad too**, as he can often be forgotten after pregnancy loss.

- **Cry with the family**. Expressing your own emotions is both healing and validating for couples facing loss. Do not feel the need to be 'strong' for the parents. They will find comfort in your honest emotions.

- **Offer to do something specific**. Bring over dinner, wash clothes, run errands, or ask if you can watch remaining children. Often times couples are told to 'call me if you need anything.' However, they can be too caught up in grief to make requests that would make their daily routines easier.

- **Acknowledge the baby**. Validating the child's existence is very important for a couple who has suffered pregnancy loss. Remember anniversary dates such as the day the baby died and the due date, as these can be very difficult times for parents. Making a charitable donation in the child's name can also be a thoughtful way to remember the baby.

- **Offer help with baby items**. If needed, assist with returning maternity items or holding baby items until the couple is ready to make decisions. When offering this type of assistance, be extremely careful to follow the parents' wishes.

- **Be patient**. Long after friends and family members have dealt with the loss and moved on, parents may still be in the depths of grief. Keep in mind that each person heals at a different pace. Parents will not just 'get over' the loss of a child. It will be a part of them throughout their lives.

- **Write a note or send a card.** Expressing genuine sympathy is helpful for those facing loss. A thoughtful letter or card can be reread over time and serve as a reminder that you care.

- **Allow honest emotions.** Be able to handle tears or strong expressions of guilt or anger from grieving parents. Remember that feeling the pain of loss is an important step toward healing. Crying and venting are healthy and they can serve as a release during grief. There is no need to try and remove the pain, simply make yourself available during difficult times.

- **Know when to ask for help.** If a grieving parent is caught in the grips of depression or intense grief for an extended period of time, seek help. A trained counselor, pastor, or support group can offer great support. However, if you suspect any suicidal thoughts or behavior, dial 911 immediately.

- **Provide information**. Offer parents a book or website such as www.HopeXchange.com, that gives insight on grief and pregnancy loss. See the *Resource* section at the back of this book for listings.

- **Offer encouragement.** A couple facing loss may tend to withdraw from the people and activities they enjoy. Offer gentle reminders of hobbies and friends the couple has shared in the past. Give rides to meetings, take them to the movies, or just get them out of the house.

- **Look toward the future.** It can be helpful for the couple to begin to plan again for the family and future they dream of. However, be very cautious when encouraging parents to have another baby. Remember that it will take time before they are ready to think about trying again.

- **Expect change.** Realize that parents dealing with pregnancy loss have been affected in various ways, and their lives have been altered. Grief can bring sorrow and strain to individuals as well as their marriages. On the other hand, it can also cause personal growth and maturity for the couple and their relationship.

Helping friends or family members deal with the pain of pregnancy loss can be challenging, but it often brings you closer. Offering support to someone in grief can be a growth experience for you both. Embrace the part you play in helping grieving parents, you will all reap the rewards.

How Can I Help the Baby's Siblings?

Children can often be overlooked during the heartache of pregnancy loss. As parents struggle to face their grief, they often have difficulty offering support to their remaining children. Velicia recounted her struggle:

"At that point I had two other children...I gave control (not legally) but more in action, to my mother and sister-in-law."

Children who have lost an expected brother or sister will face a loss of their own. They will have questions and experience fears and confusion. They will need hugs, reassurance, and extra attention during this difficult time. Velicia explained her children's eventual reaction to their loss:

"At some point the children began to ask about him [the baby]. That was really wonderful of them...in their innocence, I think they provided the support I had needed so many years ago."

As a friend or family member, your assistance with remaining children can offer a needed hand for parents that are under the strain of grief. Here are some ways you can help:

- **Encourage questions.** Allow children the freedom they need to ask questions and talk openly about the baby. Answer questions in simple and honest terms that are appropriate for the child's age and maturity level.

- **Spend time with the children.** Children need special attention during this difficult time. Parents who are in the depths of grief may not be able to meet the child's need for extra attention.

- **Offer reassurance.** A child can become confused or even fearful after the death of an expected brother or sister. They may wonder if the same thing could happen to them, and they may even feel responsible for the stress their parents are feeling.

- **Be patient.** Children facing grief may 'act out.' They can feel angry one day, and sad the next. These are healthy and normal reactions. Inform teachers and caregivers so they will be aware of the child's loss.

- **Remember the baby.** Help children to remember the baby through talking, drawing pictures, or even making a card or planting a flower.

Offering your care and support for children who have been affected by pregnancy loss can be a wonderful support for the entire family. It will provide much needed attention for the child, while easing the strain for parents dealing with their own grief.

Questions to Ask Yourself

As you support your friends or family members, here are some questions to consider:

- **Am I avoiding the couple?** Why?
- **Have I been there to listen without judging?** Am I able to listen without offering my viewpoint or advice?
- **Have I acknowledged the baby?** Am I allowing the parents to talk about the baby? If not, why?

If these questions have identified any focus areas, decide on two actions you will take to address them.

Use this space to write them down:

"Loss makes artists of us all as we weave new patterns in the fabric of our lives."
~ *Greta W. Crosby*

Chapter 16

Trying Again

*T*he decision to have another baby after suffering a miscarriage can be a very tough one to make. One minute you may feel like getting pregnant immediately, and the next minute you feel that you could never try again. The decision is an important one that only you and your partner can make.

I struggled with the decision myself, and felt weighed down by my family's well-intentioned prodding to try again. The loss of my baby made me realize how much I desperately wanted a family of my own. Although my loved ones meant well, I felt burdened by their constant reminders that my mission, to this point, had failed.

My husband's gentle advice to 'get back on the horse' was something I knew inside, but had difficulty facing. I was terrified of trying again- and losing again.

The deciding factor for me was a conversation I had with a friend who had also had a miscarriage. She had recently become pregnant again, so I decided to go to her for advice.

When I asked her how she overcame her fear (of trying again), I was shocked when she replied, " I didn't... I'm still terrified every day."

It was at that moment I realized that I was not going to 'get rid of' the fear – I had to go on in spite of it. One month later I became pregnant for the second time.

Should We Try Again?

Only you and your partner can decide what is right for you. A miscarriage may strengthen your determination to have a family, or it may cause you to question if you can handle another attempt at pregnancy.

Take the time that is needed to fully consider what you want to do and discuss it with your spouse. Realize that you and your family, or even your partner, may not agree. When Velicia decided she wanted to try again, she found that her partner had a different view:

"My fiancé was perfectly happy raising my three children as his own and did not want more babies, although I still had a twinge to right what was wronged for me...to be successful one more time having a baby."

For some couples the decision is difficult, while for others it is a non-issue. Anna shared:

" I really felt pretty hopeful from early on that our 'time could come,' that we would have our baby and it would be okay."

It is up to you and your spouse to decide what is right. If you have battled infertility or had a number of losses you should seriously consider if you can handle another try.

During my second pregnancy, I told my husband that if it did not work out I would like to adopt. I knew that my heart could not take another miscarriage. You have to know yourself and decide what is right for you.

When Should We Try Again?

There are many different schools of thought on how soon you should try again. It is important to consider your physical and emotional readiness.

Physical Readiness

Most experts and doctors agree that a woman who has suffered a miscarriage should wait at least one normal menstrual cycle before attempting to become pregnant. There is some evidence to suggest that failing to wait for one normal cycle increases the risk of miscarriage in the next pregnancy. Some doctors will suggest waiting for two to three normal cycles to ensure that your body has fully recovered.

It is important that you consult with your doctor to determine the proper wait time for you and your body. Together you can decide when you are healthy and ready to try again. Be sure that you have a supportive doctor that is meeting your needs and willing to give you the 'specialized' attention that you will need.

If you will require any additional medical attention, such as genetic counseling, be sure to seek that out before trying again. Having all the information you need is vital in helping you to make the choices and decisions ahead.

This is a time to take especially good care of you! Be sure to practice healthy eating habits and get plenty of rest and exercise.

Emotional Readiness

Emotional readiness is much more difficult to determine, and in many ways, even more critical than physical readiness.

If you find yourself hurriedly trying to become pregnant again, you may not be taking the time to properly address your grief. During a time when emotions are running high, this can be dangerous. Quickly attempting to replace your sorrow with another child may prevent you from dealing with the loss. Many women find themselves grieving (over a pregnancy loss) long after the birth of their babies.

If your focus becomes trying again, it could delay the grief and healing process and put that part of your life on hold. Also, if you fail to become pregnant right away, it can cause a feeling of failure and add to the emotions you are dealing with.

Even if you believe that you 'feel fine,' and you do not feel overwhelming effects from your loss, there is still grief. Many parents find that their pain intensifies in the months that follow their miscarriage. Most doctors agree that dealing with grief is important before trying again.

Hormonal balance may also be affected by a miscarriage. This can wreak havoc on your emotions and leave you more open to experiencing anxiety during your pregnancy.

On the other hand, if you find the months stretching on and you are still afraid to try again, it may be time to face the music. You will not be able to move forward without feeling fear. Becoming pregnant again can help you to feel that you are 'moving on' and progressing toward your dream of starting or adding to your family.

The difficulty is that the joyful anticipation you once felt about becoming pregnant has now become irreparably damaged. You will never be able to return to an untarnished view of pregnancy.

The important thing is that you take the time you need to become emotionally ready. That does not mean that you will awake one day without any fears or reservations. It simply means that you have allowed yourself to grieve and begin healing from the loss you suffered. This will open the way to try again when you are emotionally and physically ready.

What Are Our Chances?

The great news about trying again is that the odds are in your favor. After one miscarriage, the risks of another miscarriage during the next pregnancy are approximately 21%, according to the American Journal of Perinatology. After two or three, the risks are 26% and 35% (respectively). The chances with no prior miscarriage are about 20%.

Even for women who have had multiple miscarriages, the odds of having a healthy baby next time are still on their side, especially if they receive good medical care and plenty of emotional support.

Many women have more than one miscarriage during their lifetime. About 1 in 36 women have two miscarriages with no explanation at all. Any more than two, and your doctor will most likely recommend tests to rule out any specific reasons that may be causing your miscarriages. If you feel concerned, talk with your OB/GYN doctor about any next steps that may be needed.

Can I Improve My Chances?

Remember that the most common reasons for a miscarriage cannot be helped or prevented. However, it is always important to practice a healthy lifestyle while you are trying to become pregnant.

Exercise, a healthy diet, getting weight within normal limits, and reducing your stress will not only improve your health, they will also improve fertility and give you something to focus on. Limiting alcohol, quitting smoking, and taking folic acid are also great ways to prepare yourself for another pregnancy.

When You Become Pregnant Again

Becoming pregnant after a loss results in a roller coaster ride of emotions. You will feel a sense of moving on and of hope. At the same time, you may feel intense fear and worry that you could miscarry again.

Taking charge of your care during this time will help you to overcome the anxiety you feel. Here are some suggestions:

- **Get prenatal care right away!** This is even more critical if you have had more than one miscarriage. Make sure that your doctor understands your situation and is willing to help and reassure you. Consider changing doctors if needed.
- **Request an early blood test** to check your hCG and progesterone levels.
- **Have an ultrasound** at seven weeks to see the baby's heartbeat.
- **Have a Doppler heartbeat check** after the thirteenth week to hear the baby's heartbeat, and request one *anytime* you feel worried.
- **Take all the normal health precautions** you would during any other pregnancy. Take folic acid, eat healthy, drink lots of water, reduce stress, and get plenty of rest. Also, be sure to stop smoking, limit alcohol, and avoid illegal drugs.
- **Take it as easy as you can**, especially for the first three months. Let the housework go a little, keep non-critical activities to a minimum, and get help from others whenever possible.
- **Take time to relax**. Listen to relaxing music, get a massage, or just go for a walk.

Taking these steps will not prevent you from feeling anxious, but they will help! The more you can focus on your health and the part you play, the more empowered you feel. Anna explained:

> *"When I became pregnant again, I wanted to do EVERYTHING 'by the book.' A lot of my friends had beverages that included caffeine, etc., but I just didn't want to take the risk. If it happened again, I didn't want it to be MY fault or something I did. So I followed ALL the 'rules,' to a tee."*

Keep in mind that no matter how hard you try, you are still going to feel anxious and that is perfectly normal. Your goal is to keep your focus on other things and off of the possibility that you will have another miscarriage.

Coping With Fear

Even if your pregnancy is going very well, it is not uncommon to struggle with fear. Stress is an unfortunate part of a pregnancy following a miscarriage.

I found myself incredibly overwhelmed with fear during my second pregnancy. I tried to enjoy the experience, and I put on a smile for my friends and family, but inside I was completely terrified. I actually delayed naming the baby, decorating her room, and buying baby clothes because I was so afraid something would go wrong. I thought that would just make me feel worse.

I had all of the early tests; they all came back perfect. The baby had perfect ultrasounds and perfect heartbeats, but I was still petrified. At times I actually felt like a failure for being so afraid. I prayed and relied heavily on my faith, but I was still scared.

Kathy described a similar experience, recalling:

" I was worried that I may have another miscarriage, so we did not tell anyone that I was expecting...We wanted to wait until the third month had passed and things were moving along."

It is okay to feel anxious, and it is unlikely that anyone around you will relate to what you may be experiencing. When you are facing fear, it can be a rough road, but there are things you can do to help reduce it.

Here are some suggestions:

- **Take good care of yourself!** Do not overdo your activities in an effort to take your mind of off your fears; it will only wear you out.
- **Remind yourself of the facts**. Remember that you are NOT at an increased risk of miscarriage, just because you had one. Tell yourself repeatedly, until you believe it.
- **Keep in mind that the risk of miscarriage decreases as the pregnancy progresses**. There is a dramatic decrease after the eighth week goes by.

- **Bring any concern (no matter how small) to your doctor.** If you need a heartbeat test to reassure yourself, ask for one.
- **Talk to someone you trust about your fear.** If you feel your family or friends may not understand, find a pastor, support worker, or counselor who can.
- **Stay as positive as possible!** Make room for thoughts about your baby, your growing family, and the excitement of a newborn.
- **Write down a positive thought** or scripture each morning, and repeat it throughout the day.

Remember that constant stress and fear are not good for you or the baby. It is important to get the physical and emotional support you will need during this critical time.

The way you handle your pregnancy is in your hands. You can have nine months full of worry and fear or you can work towards being hopeful and expectant, the choice is yours.

Consider All of the Options

Whether you have had one pregnancy loss, or many, you may reach the decision not to become pregnant again. If your desire to have a family remains, consider all of the options that are available to loving parents.

Although most couples long to have a child of their own, adoption and foster parenting can be excellent opportunities to provide loving homes for children who desperately need them. Velicia explained that:

"My grandmother lost [a baby] in her early forties, and had a house full of foster children as a result."

If you feel any doubts about how you can connect with a child that is not your biological offspring- don't. As a stepmother and a mom, I can assure you that my heart knows no difference between my stepdaughter and my daughter. The depth of my feelings for them is equal and unaffected by biology. It is love that ties your hearts and lives together, not science.

Remember that there is nothing easier than loving a child. Consider all of the ways that parents and children can come together.

It Is Worth It

Looking back, I know that I cheated myself out of some of the early joys and happiness of having a baby. But I do know one thing, it was so worth it.

The day my daughter was born was one of the happiest and most profound I have ever had. Only my wedding day shares the greatness of that day. Finally, my fear was gone and I eagerly awaited the meeting I had longed for and dreamed of for so long; meeting my baby girl.

It was everything I had hoped for and more. I knew the instant I held her that everything I had gone through was worth it. I knew that I would do it all again without hesitation to have her.

Anna described it this way:

> *"I'm so grateful to have my little boy now. He is a joy, and I know that I'm blessed to have him. I have a very close friend who was never able to get pregnant. When I feel sad, I think about her, and so many others, who have never been able to get pregnant. I think I'm one of the lucky ones."*

I still think about a chance meeting I had at work one day, after I overheard a young woman talking to a friend. She had recently had a miscarriage, and she was pregnant again. She talked about how afraid she was, and she said she was not going to tell anyone about her pregnancy this time.

My heart went out to her. I had felt the same way just months before. I felt compelled to talk with her because I knew how few people really understand.

I told her that I had a miscarriage as well, and just had a baby. I said that I understood how scared she was, and

143

to be honest, it was not going to go away. But if she would just hang in there... it is so worth it.

She replied, " You have no idea how much I needed to hear that." That was one of events that prompted me to write this book.

It is so worth it!

Questions to Ask Yourself

As you face or experience another pregnancy, consider the following questions:
- **Am I physically and emotionally ready** to try again? If not, why?
- **Can I handle another try?** Have I considered all of my options?
- **Am I feeling anxious or afraid?** Why? What will I do about it?

Have you considered trying again? Write about it now:

_____

_____

_____

_____

_____

_____

_____

_____

_____

_____

If the questions you have just answered identified areas that you would like to change or focus on, decide on two to three actions you will take to address them.

Use this space to write them down:

_____

_____

_____

_____

_____

_____

_____

_____

_____

_____

_____

_____

_____

_____

_____

_____

_____

_____

_____

_____

_____

" We could never learn to be brave and patient, if there were only joy in the world."
~ Helen Keller

Chapter 17

Finding Meaning in Your Loss

*I*t is impossible to walk through the dark days of grief without feeling changed. You will not emerge from your loss as the same person who began. Conquering grief and surviving loss stretches you, tests you, and takes you to the very brink of your endurance.

Coming out on the other side of grief is a triumph as well as a loss of innocence. It may change your views about yourself, your marriage, death, and even God. It is life changing.

After experiencing a traumatic loss we often feel the need to assess what has happened. It is helpful and even necessary to find the meaning in our loss.

The painful journey through grief is one that often causes tremendous personal growth. A discovery of personal strength and courage can arise from the depths of loss. Velicia explained:

"Now it's not so bad as I understand that [my baby] Shelby's coming and going was a lesson in growth."

It can be good to step back and assess how the loss affected your personal growth. You may not have felt it possible to make it through such a traumatic experience, and yet you have. That alone is a great personal accomplishment.

You may still struggle with understanding the reason your loss occurred, that is only human. It is important to keep in mind that death and loss are an unfortunate part of life. We cannot prevent them from happening, but we can control how we react to them.

Some feel that there was a purpose or meaning for their loss. After my miscarriage, I felt an immediate sense that there was a reason it happened. At the time, I had no idea what it could be, but the feeling was intense and unmistakable.

I now believe that the loss of my baby was the beginning of a personal journey of examination and change. The experience caused me to reconsider my future and make changes I never expected to make. It changed the course of my life.

Anna had a similar feeling, remembering:

"From early on, I kept hearing from others and kept telling myself that it was meant to be. I thought to myself, maybe I needed to go through that. Maybe it would make me a better mother when it would be my turn. Maybe it was all part of God's plan...and who am I to question that?"

Some may feel that a higher purpose was at work in the background of their loss, while others focus on the personal growth that occurred. You may actually feel stronger in the knowledge that you conquered grief. This strength can often cause one to make decisions that may have seemed difficult, or even impossible before. Velicia described her experience by saying:

*"Today I understand that was God's way of taking care
of so many unresolved things. A failing marriage, a
pregnancy too close to the previous one, the growing of a
person into a woman who would eventually make some
drastic changes for her children and for herself."*

No matter what your personal views are, overcoming
loss should be a time of taking stock and measuring
personal growth. Spend a moment considering the positive
changes you have noticed in yourself. Consider the
confidence you now have to face whatever life hands you.
Velicia described this when she said:

*"Life does go on after loss...and it's about 'living
through' the growth enough to know that you have."*

Walking through grief can show us what really matters.
The experience will remind us that life is fragile and we
should value and enjoy every minute we have. It will teach
us not to take life or our loved ones for granted. And it will
show us what we are made of.

Questions to Ask Yourself

Consider the following questions as you think about
the meaning of your loss:
- **Do I feel there was a meaning or purpose for my
  loss?** If so, what? If not, how am I coping?
- **Did I form any new relationships or strengthen
  any existing ones?** With whom?
- **Do I tell others how I feel about them?** When?
  How? Am I more aware of the value of life?
- **Did this experience cause me to question or
  strengthen my beliefs or faith?** In what ways?
- **Am I more confident in myself now?** My
  marriage?
- **Has this experience caused me to grow as a
  person?** How?

Use these questions to identify the positive changes that resulted from dealing with your loss.

Use this space to write them down:

_____

_____

_____

_____

_____

_____

_____

_____

_____

_____

_____

_____

_____

_____

_____

_____

_____

_____

_____

Did the above questions cause you to identify areas you would like to focus on? If so, consider 2-3 actions you will take to address them.

Use this space to write them down.

_____

_____

_____

_____

_____

_____

_____

_____

_____

_____

_____

_____

_____

_____

_____

_____

_____

_____

Now it is time to consider all of the focus areas and actions you recorded throughout this book. Take time now to reflect and review all of the items you have written.

You may find that there are actions you planned that you have already completed. Congratulations! You may want to place a check mark next to those items to identify your progress.

Also examine the 'outstanding' actions you have planned, those you have not yet completed. On the next page, you will identify the five remaining actions that you feel are most important to you. Consider this as you look over the items you have written.

Based on the actions you recorded throughout the book, write down five that are most important to you:

1. _____

   _____

2. _____

   _____

3. _____

   _____

4. _____

   _____

5. _____

   _____

Now that you have narrowed your focus to five critical steps that will assist in your healing, here are some tips to help you accomplish them:

- **Prioritize**. Put your goals in order based on their importance. Start with the most important item first, and then work your way down.
- **Use your calendar**. Record your plans and goals on your calendar, planner, or PDA. Assign due dates to important items to help you stay on track.
- **Be accountable**. Ask a family member, trusted friend, or counselor to hold you accountable. Share your plans, actions, and completion dates, and ask him/her to check back with you periodically on your progress.
- **Seek progress, not perfection**. Realize that any steps you make toward healing should be recognized and rewarded.

Your journey does not stop here. Consider the improvements you have already made, and the actions you are planning.

Remember,

"Hope is like the sun, which, as we journey toward it, casts the shadow of our burden behind us." ~ *S. Smiles*

May your burdens become shadows as you journey toward hope.

Afterword

Congratulations on finishing *Hope is Like the Sun*. Although reading a book will not erase your grief, you have taken an important step towards healing. I hope these pages have brought you comfort, encouragement, and practical solutions that you can apply today.

Grief can linger and even revisit us throughout our lives, so I encourage you to keep this book handy as a reference. Visit www.HopeXchange.com and use the *Resource* section to locate books and additional websites that can provide support and information. Review the focus areas and actions you recorded from time to time to track your progress and provide an opportunity for personal reflection.

Facing loss is a life-changing event. It can cause you to be stretched in ways you never imaged, and it often leads to an examination of your personal values and beliefs. If you continue to question your beliefs or spirituality, please consider seeking the help of others. A trusted pastor, rabbi, priest, or friend may be able to offer the answers you seek. The Appendix of this book lists helpful resources under the *Religious and Inspirational* section. Remember those who seek will find.

It has often been said that the final stage of grief, the ultimate healing, is helping someone else who is grieving. I can only hope that this book has accomplished that purpose. May God bless your steps toward healing.

About the Author

Lisa Church decided to apply years of Corporate Support experience in a new direction after suffering a miscarriage. She now offers support to women and their families coping with pregnancy loss. Her website, *HopeXchange,* supplies information, articles, support, and products that offer hope and healing.

Visit *HopeXchange* at http://www.HopeXchange.com. You can also contact Lisa, who resides in Hampton, Virginia, by emailing her at Lisa@HopeXchange.com.

HopeXchange.com

Shining Light on Loss

Appendix

Resources

The books and websites below are listed to provide you with helpful resources and information. Listings are included for your reference and should not be considered personal endorsements. Notes pages have been provided for you at the end of this section.

Books from larger publishers will arrive much sooner if you shop your local bookstore or use online book services such as:
http://www.amazon.com/
http://www.booksamillion.com/
http://www.barnesandnoble.com/.

How to Order Books. You may locate the publishers ordering address and add $4.00 for air shipping. Be sure to include applicable sales tax when ordering from publishers in your state.

Miscarriage, Stillbirth, Infant Death & SIDS

Books:
A Guide for Fathers: When a Baby Dies by Tim Nelson. A Place to Remember.

Another Baby? Maybe...30 Questions on Pregnancy After Loss by Sherokee Ilse and Maribeth W. Doer. Wintergreen Press.

A Silent Sorrow: Pregnancy Loss- Guidance and Support for You and Your Family by Perry-Lynn Moffitt, Isabelle A. Wilkins and Ingrid Kohn. Delta.

A Woman Doctor's Guide to Miscarriage: Essential Facts and Up-To-The Minute Information on Coping With Pregnancy Loss and Trying Again by Irene Daria, Laurie Abkemeier (Editor) and Lynn Friedman. Hyperion.

Dear Parents: A Collection of Letters to Bereaved Parents edited by Joy Johnson. Centering Corporation.

Empty Arms: Coping with Miscarriage, Stillbirth and Infant Loss by Sherokee Ilse. Wintergreen Press.

Empty Cradle, Broken Heart: Surviving the Death of Your Baby by Deborah L. Davis, Ph.D. Fulcrum Publishing.

Hope is Like the Sun: Finding Hope and Healing After Miscarriage, Stillbirth, or Infant Death by Lisa Church. HopeXchange Publishing.

How to Prevent Miscarriage and Other Crisis of Pregnancy by Carol Colman and Stefan Semchyshyn. MacMillan General Reference.

Miscarriage After Infertility: A Woman's Guide to Coping by Margaret Comerford Freda EdD, RN, CHES, FAAN, and Carrie F. Semelsberger RN, BSN, BS. Fairview Press.

Miscarriage: A Man's Book by Rick Wheat. Centering Corporation.

Miscarriage: A Shattered Dream by Sherokee Ilse and Linda Hammer Burns. Wintergreen Press.

Miscarriage: Why it Happens and How Best to Reduce Your Risks. A Doctor's Guide to the Facts by Henry Lerner M.D. Perseus.

Motherhood After Miscarriage by Dr. Kathleen Diamond. Bob Adam, Inc.

Precious Lives, Painful Choices: A Prenatal Decision-Making Guide by Sherokee Ilse. Wintergreen Press.

Pregnancy After a Loss by Carol Cirulli Lanham. Berkely Books.

Still to Be Born by Pat Scheibert and Paul Kirk. Perinatal Loss.

Stories of Miscarriage – Healing with Words edited by Rachel Faldet and Karen Fitton. Fairview Press, Minneapolis.

The SIDS Survival Guide: Information and Comfort for Grieving Family & Friends & Professionals Who Seek To Help Them by Joani Nelson Horchler and Robin Rice Morris. SIDS Educational Services.

Trying Again: A Guide to Pregnancy After Miscarriage, Stillbirth and Infant Loss by Ann Douglas. Taylor Publishing.

Unsupported Losses: Ectopic Pregnancy, Molar Pregnancy, and Blighted Ovum by Sherokee Ilse. Wintergreen Press.

Websites:
A Place to Remember. Thorough site that exclusively offers infant loss materials. http://www.aplacetoremember.com

A Quiet Refuge. Remembrance albums and items for families who suffer pregnancy loss or infant death.
http://www.quietrefuge.com/home.cfm

Angel Babies Forever Loved. Grief information along with keepsake ideas and helpful hints for family members.
http://www.angels4ever.com/

Centering Corporation. Bereavement resource offering books, newsletters, and infant loss resources.
http://www.centering.org/

Facts About Miscarriage. Contains information, bulletin boards and a remembrance page. http://www.pregnancyloss.info/

Fertility Plus. Includes an extensive list of miscarriage support resources.
http://www.fertilityplus.org/faq/miscarriage/resources.html

First Candle. SIDS, stillbirth, and early infant death resources, training, fundraising ideas, and support.
http://www.firstcandle.org

HopeXchange. Support, information, articles, books, message boards and resources for anyone impacted by miscarriage, stillbirth or infant death. http://www.hopexchange.com

Miscarriage Information Page. Answers to FAQs written by an M.D.http://web.ukonline.co.uk/Members/ruth.livingstone/little/miscarri.htm

Miscarriage Support Auckland Inc. New Zealand based website offering information and email support.
http://www.miscarriagesupport.org.nz/

Remembering Our Babies. Includes information on Pregnancy and Infant Loss Remembrance Day.
http://www.pregnancyandinfantloss.com/

Silent Grief. Offers daily healing thoughts, chat boards and encouragement. http://www.silentgrief.com/

Texas Moms of Tiny Angels. Includes Memorial Garden and a chat site. http://www.txmomsoftinyangels.org/index2.htm

Wintergreen Press. Offers a wide range of books and booklets on miscarriage and infant death. http://www.wintergreenpress.com

National Organizations & Support Groups

Websites:
Abiding Hearts. Resource for parents in pregnancies that have revealed birth defects. Telephone: 406-293-4416 Website:
http://www.asfhelp.com/ASF_files/support_group_files/abiding
_heart_files/Abiding_Hearts_Home.htm

AGAST Alliance of Grandparents. Support for grandparents who have lost a grandchild. Telephone: 1-800-793-7437 Website:
http://www.agast.org/

American SIDS Institute. Provides information and research on SIDS (Sudden Infant Death Syndrome). Telephone: 1-800-232-SIDS Website: http://www.sids.org/

Bereaved Parents of the USA. Offers nationwide free meetings for bereaved parents, siblings, or grandparents. Telephone: (630) 971-3490 Website: http://www.bereavedparentsusa.org/

CLIMB (Center for Loss in Multiple Birth). Parents who have experienced the death of one or more twins or higher multiples. Telephone: 907-222-5321 Website:
http://www.climbsupport.org/enabled/index.html

The Compassionate Friends. A nationwide network of seasoned grievers reaching out to the newly bereaved. Telephone: 877-969-0010 Website: http://www.compassionatefriends.org/

The Hygeia Foundation. A global community offering programs, support, and message boards on pregnancy loss. Website:
http://www.hygeia.org/

The MISS Foundation (Mothers in Sympathy and Support).
Provides immediate and ongoing support to grieving families.
P.O. Box 5333 Peoria, AZ 85385-5333 Website:
http://www.misschildren.org/index.html

National SIDS Resource Center. Provides information services and
technical assistance on SIDS (Sudden Infant Death Syndrome)
and related topics. Telephone: 1-866- 866-7437 Website:
http://www.sidscenter.org/

PATH (Parents Available To Help). A network of parents of
premature babies and special needs children who have endured
a high-risk pregnancy. Telephone: 1-800-399-7284 Website:
http://www.birth23.org/Resources/ParentsAvailable.asp

*Pregnancy Loss Support Program: National Council of Jewish
Women- NY Section*. Offers free telephone counseling and
conducts support groups in the NY area. Telephone: 212- 687-
5030 ext. 28 Website: http://www.ncjwny.org/services_plsp.htm

SHARE Pregnancy and Infant Loss Support. Support for those
who have suffered pregnancy loss, stillbirth, or newborn death.
Telephone: 800-821-6819 Website:
http://www.nationalshareoffice.com/

SPALS (Subsequent Pregnancy After a Loss Support*)*. Email
message boards for those who suffered pregnancy loss and are
considering or experiencing a subsequent pregnancy. Website:
http://www.spals.com/home/index.html

Magazines & Newsletters

Abiding Hearts. A newsletter for parents who choose to carry a
baby with a genetic defect to term. Telephone: (406) 293-4416
Website:
http://www.asfhelp.com/ASF_files/support_group_files/abiding
_heart_files/Abiding_Hearts_Home.htm

The AGAST Newsletter. Information for grandparents who have
lost a grandchild. Telephone: 1-800-793-7437 Website:
http://www.agast.org/newsltr/index.html

Alive Alone. A newsletter for parents whose child has died. 11115
Dull Robinson Road Van Wert, OH. 45891 Website:
http://www.alivealone.org/

Bereavement Magazine. A magazine of hope and healing. Telephone: 1-888- 60-4HOPE Website: http://www.bereavementmag.com/

Fernside Inside. Newsletter for grieving children. Telephone: (513) 745-0111 Website: http://www.fernside.org/about/newsletter.html

Grief Digest. Magazine featuring articles on bereavement. Telephone: (402) 553-1200 Website: http://www.centering.org/membership.htm

Hannah to Hannah. Newsletter with Christian emphasis that covers infertility or the loss of a child. Telephone: (775) 852-9202 Website: http://www.hannah.org/ministries/h2h.htm

M.E.N.D. Newsletter. Christian-based information for women who have experienced miscarriage. Telephone: 1- 888-695-MEND Website: http://www.mend.org/news_online.asp

Our Newsletter. For parents who experienced loss during twin or multiple pregnancy. Telephone: (907) 222-5321 Website: http://www.climb-support.org/

SHARE Newsletter. For parents who have experienced pregnancy loss or infant death. Telephone: 1-800-821-6819 Website: http://www.nationalshareoffice.com/newsletter.asp

Sidelines Customized Newsletter. Information on high-risk pregnancies. Telephone: 1-888-447-4754 Website: http://www.sidelines.org/

We Need Not Walk Alone Magazine. Offers grief support for families who have experienced the death of a child. Telephone: 630-990-0010 Website: ***http://www.compassionatefriends.org/wnnwa_index.shtml***

Religious and Inspirational

Books:
A Grief Observed by C.S. Lewis. Harper SanFrancisco.

Good Grief by Granger Westberg. Fortress Press.

I Can't Find a Heartbeat by Melissa Sexson Hanson. Review & Herald Pub Assn.

When Bad Things Happen to Good People by Harold Kusher. Avon.

Where is God When it Hurts? by Phillip Yancey. Zondervan.

Why Us? When Bad Things Happen to God's People by Warren Wiersbe. Baker Book House.

Websites:
A Woman's Place. Christian support and comfort for miscarriage, infertility, and special needs children. http://www.waymarks.com/wmnplc/support.html

Cross Search. Christian Miscarriage Support group providing an email list for anyone who has suffered a miscarriage. http://www.crosssearch.com/People/Women/41672.php

Hannah's Prayer Ministries. Christian support for fertility challenges or the loss of a child. http://www.hannah.org/

HopeXchange. Offers a section of Christian support and information for those dealing with pregnancy loss. http://www.HopeXchange_Inspirational.com

M.E.N.D. (Mommies Enduring Neonatal Death) Christian support, information and keepsakes. http://www.mend.org/home_index.asp

National Office of Post Abortion Reconciliation and Healing. Religious-affiliated organization providing support. http://www.noparh.org/

Open ARMs. Online Bible counseling for those healing from abortion. http://www.oaim.org/

Children and Grief

Books for Children:
I Remember You Today by Casey Curry. The Annapolis Publishing Company http://annapolisbooks.com.

Last Week My Brother Anthony Died by Martha Hickman. Abingdon Press.

Lifetime: The Beautiful Way to Explain Death to Children by Bryan Mellonie and Robert Ingpen. Bantam Doubleday Dell Publishing.

The Fall of Freddie the Leaf: A Story for All Ages by Leo Buscaglia. Henry Holt & Company, Inc.

Thumpy's Story: A Story of Love and Grief Shared by Thumpy the Bunny by Nancy C. Dodge. Prairie Lark Press.

Timothy Duck by Lynn Bennett Blackburn. Centering Corporation.

Where's Jess? by Joy and Marv Johnson. Centering Corporation.

Books for Parents and Adults:
35 Ways to Help a Grieving Child by The Dougy Center. The Dougy Center for Grieving Children.

For Those Who Live: Helping Children Cope with the Death of a Brother or Sister by Kathy La Tour. Centering Corporation.

Guiding Your Child Through Grief by Mary Ann Emswiler M.A. M.P.S. & James Emswiler. Bantam Books.

Talking About Death: A Dialogue Between Parent and Child by Earl A. Grollman. Beacon Press.

Websites:
KIDSAID website for children. http://kidsaid.com/

Raindrop. A cartoon story that explains death to children. http://iul.com/raindrop/

The Waterbug Story. A brief, beautifully written story on death-for all ages.
http://www.fortnet.org/WidowNet/poems/waterbug.htm

Keepsakes and Remembrances

Websites:
A Place to Remember. Offers cards, baby books, ornaments and jewelry designed to remember your baby.
http://www.aplacetoremember.com

Comfort Baskets. Baskets filled with items that help the healing process begin. http://www.comfortbaskets.com/

Craft Designs for You. Offers free cross stitch samplers to commemorate your baby.
http://www.craftdesigns4you.com/memory.htm

International Star Registry. Name a star in your baby's honor.
http://www.starregistry.com/

Memory Box Artist Program. Memory boxes for families of infants who die in the hospital.
http://www.craftdesigns4you.com/memory.htm

Once Upon a Name. Offers a selection of Mother's rings and bracelets and baby's name art.
http://www.onceuponaname.com/

Proud Mom Bracelets. Angelite Creations offers personalized bracelets.
http://www.angelitecreations.com/html/proud_mom_bracelets.html

Remember Me Bears. Creates keepsake teddy bears from fabric or clothing you provide.
http://www.remembermebear.com/index.htm

Depression

Websites:
American Psychiatric Association. Telephone: (703) 907-7300
http://www.psych.org/

American Psychological Association. Telephone: 1-800-374-2721
http://www.apa.org

National Alliance for the Mentally Ill. HelpLine: 1-800-950-NAMI
http://nami.org

National Depressive and Manic Depressive Association.
Telephone: 1-800-826-3622. http://www.dbsalliance.org/

National Institute of Mental Health. Telephone: 1-866-615-NIMH
http://www.nimh.nih.gov

Infertility

Websites:
Fertility Plus. Information written by patients for patients.
http://www.pinelandpress.com/toc.html

INCIID. Infertility information and support.
http://www.inciid.org

Resolve. The National Infertility Association.
http://www.resolve.org/main/national/index.jsp?name=home

General Grief

Books:
Love Never Dies. A Mother's Journey from Loss to Love by Sandy Goodman. Jodere Group, Inc. http://loveneverdies.net/

On Death and Dying by Elizabeth Kubler-Ross. Macmillan.

Tear Soup by Pat Schwiebert and Chuck DeKlyen. Perinatal Loss.

When a Man Faces Grief/A Man You Know is Grieving by James E. Miller and Thomas Golden. Willowgreen Publishing.

Websites:
Bereavement Support. Online support group for women who have suffered miscarriage.
http://www.familyvillage.wisc.edu/lib_bere.htm

Beyond Indigo. Changing the way you feel about grief and loss.
http://www.death.net/articles/article.php/artID/412

Crisis, Grief & Healing. Information and resources for men and women in grief. http://www.webhealing.com/

Dying, Grief and Mourning Resources. Provides useful links and resources.
http://home.about.com/health/mentalhealth/msub30.htm

Grief Net. Collection of resources and email chat groups.
http://griefnet.org/

Grief Watch. Information and resources for bereaved families and professional caregivers. http://www.griefwatch.com/

Resource Notes

Use the space below for notes on the books and websites that interest you.

_____

_____

_____

_____

_____

_____

_____

_____

_____

_____

_____

_____

_____

_____

_____

_____

_____

_____

_____

_____

_____

_____

_____

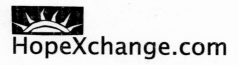

HopeXchange.com

Shining Light on Loss

Glossary

abortion- any spontaneous expulsion of a fetus before it is sufficiently developed to survive; miscarriage.

D and C (Dilation & Curettage or D&C)- a procedure in which the cervix is dilated and the lining of the uterus is scraped to remove tissue.

Doppler heartbeat check- a procedure that uses a device to produce the audible sound of fetal heartbeats.

ectopic pregnancy- a pregnancy in which the ovum (or egg) develops outside the uterus, most commonly in the Fallopian tubes. These pregnancies are not normally viable, and most require surgery.

Fetal Alcohol Syndrome- a condition affecting infants characterized by mental retardation, heart defects, physical malformations, etc., that is caused by excessive alcohol consumption during pregnancy. Less severe cases are called Fetal Alcohol Effect.

fetal demise- death of a baby in utero (inside the uterus), diagnosed by an ultrasound. Also called intrauterine fetal demise (IUFD).

grief- intense emotional suffering caused by loss, disaster, etc.

habitual aborter- a woman with several unexplained, spontaneous miscarriages.

hCG (human chorionic gonadotropin)- a hormone that stimulates the ovaries to produce other hormones that prevent menstruation. Its presence in the urine indicates pregnancy.

lupus- a chronic condition of the autoimmune system that may affect many organ systems including the skin, joints, and internal organs.

miscarriage- pregnancy loss that occurs during the first 20 weeks of pregnancy.

mourning- the external expression of grief or sorrow.

Perinatology- the study of the period of time closely surrounding birth.

progesterone- a hormone that is active in preparing the uterus to receive and develop a fertilized egg and the mammary glands for milk secretion.

Scleroderma- a soft tissue disorder (often caused by an auto-immune disease) that affects the internal organs and causes the skin to stiffen and thicken.

SIDS (Sudden Infant Death Syndrome)- the sudden death of an apparently healthy infant, of unknown cause, but thought to be related to respiratory control.

spontaneous abortion- a medical term for any sudden miscarriage.

stillbirth- pregnancy loss occurring after the 20th week of pregnancy.

therapeutic abortion- an elective procedure that terminates a pregnancy.

threatened abortion- when bleeding occurs during pregnancy, and a miscarriage may be forthcoming.

ultrasound- the use of ultrasonic waves to form images of interior body organs such as the uterus.

Index

HopeXchange.com

Shining Light on Loss

Order Form

Email Orders: Email your order to
Lisa@HopeXchange.com
Telephone Orders: Call 757-826-2162
Postal Orders: Mail this order form to:

HopeXchange Publishing
26 Towne Centre Way #731
Hampton, VA. 23666-1999

Please send the following Book/s. I understand that I
may return them for a full refund.

_____

_____

_____

_____

Please send me FREE information on:
_____ Free Newsletter   _____ Mailing List   _____ Speaking

Name:_____

Address:_____

City:_____ State:_____

Zip:_____ Email Address:_____

Sales Tax: Please add 4.5% sales tax to all products
shipped to Virginia addresses.

Payment: _____ Money Order   _____ Certified Check

Pay online with your credit card. Visit *HopeXchange* on
the web at:

http://www.HopeXchange.com

HopeXchange.com

Shining Light on Loss

Order Form

Email Orders: Email your order to
Lisa@HopeXchange.com
Telephone Orders: Call 757-826-2162
Postal Orders: Mail this order form to:

HopeXchange Publishing
26 Towne Centre Way #731
Hampton, VA. 23666-1999

Please send the following Book/s. I understand that I
may return them for a full refund.

_____

_____

_____

_____

Please send me FREE information on:
____ Free Newsletter   ____ Mailing List   ____ Speaking

Name:_____

Address:_____

City:_____ State:_____

Zip:_____ Email Address:_____

Sales Tax: Please add 4.5% sales tax to all products
shipped to Virginia addresses.

Payment: _____ Money Order   _____ Certified Check

Pay online with your credit card. Visit *HopeXchange* on
the web at:

 http://www.HopeXchange.com